D0500997

INDIAN
REGIONAL COOKING

INDIAN
REGIONAL COOKING

SUMANA RAY

CHARTWELL
BOOKS, INC.

A *Quill* BOOK

Published by
CHARTWELL BOOKS, INC.
A Division of Book Sales, Inc.
110 Enterprise Avenue
Secaucus, New Jersey 07094

© Quill Publishing Limited 1986

ISBN 01-89009-940-5

All rights reserved
No part of this publication may be reproduced, stored in a retrieval system, or
transmitted, in any form or by any means without the prior permission in writing
of the publisher and copyright holder, nor be otherwise circulated in any form of
binding or cover other than that in which it is published and without a similar
condition, including this condition, being imposed on the subsequent purchaser.

This book was designed and produced by
Quill Publishing Limited
he Old Brewery, 6 Blundell Street, London N7 9BH

Senior Editor *Patricia Webster*
Editors *Liz Davies Emma Foa Jane Laing*
Designer *Alex Arthur*
Photographer *Michael Freeman*
Illustrator *Lorraine Harrison*
Paste up *Patrizio Semproni*
Indexer *Hilary Bird*

Art Director *Nigel Osborne*
Editorial Director *Jim Miles*

The author would like to thank the following for help with recipes: Mrs Asthana,
Mrs Anju Bhaya, Mrs Noreen Bobb, Ms Sukirta Chopra, Mrs Kalpana Pal
Chouduri, Mrs Meera Chouduri, Mrs Mamta Gupta, Mrs Jacobs, Mrs Malati
Kothari, Mrs Girija Lakshmanan, Ms Devika Makhijani, Mrs Jharna Sen, Mrs
Purnima Sonti, Mrs Vatcha, Mrs Gurupdesh Verma. Thanks also to the following
for help with photography: The Beagle Gallery, London W2; Muriel Ghosh,
Pamela Marks, Diane Maxfield, Mary McKenzie. And for typing, Wendy Vincent.

Special thanks are due to Neyla Freeman, Maya Sen,
Rupa Sen, Gouri Sengupta and, above all, Sujon Ray

Filmset by Context Typesetting, Brighton, England
and QV Typesetting Ltd, London, England
Colour origination by Hong Kong Graphic Arts Limited, Hong Kong
Printed and bound by Leefung-Asco Printers Limited, Hong Kong

CONTENTS

INTRODUCTION

To many people outside India, Indian food means just curry. Indeed, many of the dishes now popular in the West are delicious and fiery curries such as the Goan favorite, vindaloo. Food is, however, a celebrated item all over India and you do not need to delve too deeply into the subject to discover that there is a stunning array of dishes, some steamed, some fried, some broiled; some subtle and delicate, some full-bodied and rich to reflect the great diversity of the country.

There is no one India and no one Indian cuisine. It is a vast country of more than one and a half million square miles of changing topography and more than seven hundred million people of various faiths.

Although modern ease of transport has, to some extent, blurred the distinction between the states, there are still real differences separating, for instance, the meat-eating North from the largely vegetarian South, the fish-eating East from the vegetarian West.

The cuisine of Northern India has been greatly influenced by the Moghuls who invaded India in the eighth century. The Moghuls enjoyed meat (but not pork, which was forbidden by their religion), poultry, ghee, nuts and saffron, and so most of the elaborate meat dishes come from the North of the country. In the South very little meat is eaten, and rice plays a large part in the diet: rice cakes or rice and lentil pancakes are typical dishes. The abundance of coconut trees in this part of the country means it is the characteristic flavor.

For the purposes of this book, India has been divided into five sections: the North comprises Kashmir and Punjab; the South, Andhra Pradesh, Tamil Nadu, Karnataka and Kerala; the Center, Rajasthan, Madhya Pradesh, Bihar and Uttar Pradesh; the East, Bengal, Orissa and Assam; the West, Gujarat and Maharashtra. There are separate sections for rice and breads, and accompaniments. Finally, there is a section on dishes that were influenced by the many foreigners who came to invade or to settle in India.

There are many Parsees from Persia and Jews from Armenia who have settled in India; typical dishes are, respectively, Fish with eggs and Chicken with beets. Goa, on the west coast of India, was under Portuguese rule until 1961 and this fact is reflected in such dishes as Shrimp vindaloo. The inheritance from the British includes such Raj dishes as Chicken jhal frezie and Mulligatawny soup. There are still many colonial clubs in India where, for dinner, you would be served a soup; then fish either fried, baked or broiled; then rice or pilaf with a meat curry; and finally a dessert.

Indian customs

Indians are known for their hospitality. If you go to an Indian home for a meal and do not have three or four helpings, they will think you have not enjoyed yourself. Indians eat with their fingers and use only their right hand. Traditionally, a small mat is placed on the floor for each person and the guests and the men of the house are asked to be seated. Each person has their food arranged in small bowls on a thali (a large metallic tray), which is brought to them. All the different dishes, including the dessert, are served at the same time.

Alternatively, you might eat from a banana leaf and the ladies of the house would serve everybody. If you were to go to an orthodox house you would not be allowed into the kitchen because you might bring in germs. In modern times, however, people do sit around the table for meals and eat from china plates, but most still use their fingers to eat.

For any happy occasion and for certain festivals, Indians will distribute sweetmeats to their relatives and friends. When my son was born in England, my parents distributed sweetmeats in Calcutta.

Planning an Indian meal

An Indian meal is not divided into different courses. An informal, non-vegetarian meal will consist of rice and/or chappati (flat bread), a dal (lentil dish), a vegetable, meat, pickles, a yogurt accompaniment and a dessert. A vegetarian meal would include two vegetable dishes. For a party, increase the number of dishes.

Indian food can be prepared in advance and warmed up in the oven just before the mealtime. Most Indian foods freeze very well with the exception of potatoes, which tend to go soggy.

In India there is no curry powder; for each recipe you mix whatever spices you require. The spices can be used whole, ground, or roasted and ground. The Indian housewife is likely to have at least twenty-five different spices in her kitchen, many of which she has grown herself. No two combinations are the same and she mixes them with the skill of an artist mixing colors on a palette.

Indian cooking offers great flexibility, for when you have some experience you can increase or decrease the quantity of the spices to your taste. You can also try adding different spices or making up completely new dishes. Even the more traditional dishes vary greatly from cook to cook.

Serve raitas and rice or bread with very hot dishes — this is much more refreshing than water.

The recipes in this book will serve four to six people. If you have many people coming, increase the number of dishes rather than the quantities, so that you can offer a greater variety of flavors.

THE INDIAN PANTRY

Spices

Spices are the main ingredients for Indian cookery. Whole spices have a different taste from ground spices, and when the spices are dry roasted, they taste entirely different again. Simple dishes may have just one or two spices, whereas more elaborate dishes might involve ten or twelve. By adding different spices for the baghar phoron, the entire taste of the dish can be changed.

In India, spices are normally bought whole and then ground for daily use on a grinding stone with a little water. If spices are required to be ground dry, a mortar and pestle is used. In the modern kitchen, the spices can easily be ground in an electric coffee grinder, so long as you make sure that you do not overheat it.

Spices can be bought ready ground but these have to be stored in airtight jars as they lose their flavor very quickly.

As Indian cookery has become popular, more and more spices are easily available. Supermarkets sell many of the spices you will need, but for a few special ones you will have to make a trip to an Indian grocery store.

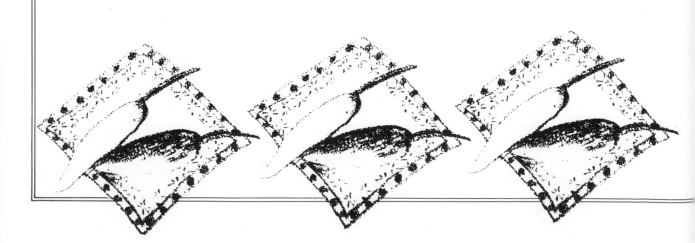

In Indian cooking, onions, coconut, poppy seeds and almonds are some of the thickening agents. Normally the spices are cooked a little before the meat, fish or vegetables are added so that you get all the flavor.

Asafetida (*Hing*) A strong smelling gum resin found in Afghanistan and Kashmir. It comes in varying colors from pale yellow to dark brown, depending on the plant it came from. It is sold in pieces or in ground form. It is popular in India as a digestive and is used in small amounts only. A pinch is added to hot oil and allowed to sizzle for a few seconds before the other ingredients are added.

Black cumin seeds (*Shah jeera*) These are smaller than the ordinary cumin seeds and dark in color.

Black salt (*Kala namak*) This is a rock salt with a distinctive flavor. It is used in small quantities in chutneys, pickles and snacks.

Cardamom (*Elaichi*) There are two kinds of cardamom used in India. The large cardamoms (bada elaichi) have black pods with black seeds inside and a strong flavor. The small cardamoms (choota elaichi) have greenish colored pods with black seeds and a pleasant aroma. These are used widely in Indian cooking. When the recipe calls for cardamoms, take the whole, small cardamoms and, just before using, press the cardamom on a hard surface with your thumb and forefinger to break the skin, so that the flavor mixes with the other ingredients while cooking.

Ground cardamom is available in Indian grocery stores or supermarkets, but cardamoms can be ground easily in an electric coffee grinder. When grinding, remove the seeds from the pods and grind just the seeds. Alternatively, grind the whole pod finely, put the powdered spice on a plate and blow gently on it — the skin is so light that it will be blown away.

Chili, dried red (*Lal mirchi*) Available in whole or ground form. The whole chilies, when added to hot oil and fried for a few seconds, turn darker in color and give a lovely flavor to the dish. (If you are not used to doing this, open the door or window because sometimes the fumes irritate the throat and make you cough.) If you do not want the dish hot, remove the seeds by cutting the skin. Make sure you wash your hands thoroughly after handling chilies as the oil on your fingers will tend to cause a burning sensation if you touch your eyes.

Cinnamon (*Dalchini*) This is the dried inner bark of the cinnamon tree. It is mainly used whole in rice, meat and fish dishes for its aroma and flavor.

Cloves (*Laung*) This is the flower bud of the clove tree and when dried it is used as a spice. Cloves also contain essential oils. They are used whole in rice and meat dishes for their aroma and flavor.

Coriander, fresh (*Hara dhaniya*) This is also known as Chinese parsley or cilantro. It is used in small amounts to garnish or added towards the end of the cooking time for its aroma; it is also used for

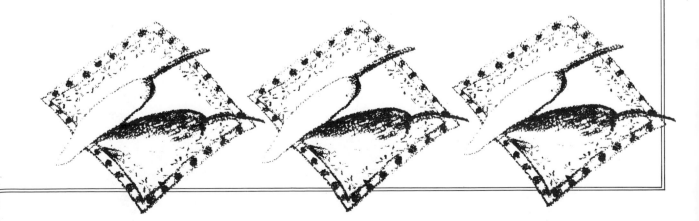

Ground chili

Cumin seed

Onion seed

Ground cumin

Dried chilies

Bay leaves

Poppy seed

Ground coriander

Coriander seed

Mustard seed

Small cardamoms

Fenugreek

Ground turmeric

Ground asafetida

Stick cinnamon

Ground mustard

Above *Fragrant mountains of vibrant color characterize the spice merchant's store. Shopping for spices is a delightful task.*

Left *Panch phoron is a combination of five spices, used in the preparation of lentil and vegetable dishes.*

making chutney. It can be grown easily in your garden or window box from the dried seeds. Place the seeds in soil about 1 in deep and keep well watered. They should start to sprout within a week to ten days. Let them grow for about ten days and then use only the top leaves and they will keep growing back. Alternatively, buy them at an Indian grocer's. For garnishing, use only the leaves. For chutneys you can use the upper stalks with the leaves and throw away the lower, thicker stalks and the roots.

Coriander, seeds (*Dhaniya*) The seeds are small and round in shape and beige in color. Ground coriander is used a great deal in cooking vegetables and meats. This is the main ingredient in commercially prepared curry powder.

Cumin (*Jeera*) Like caraway seeds, but with a slightly pungent flavor. Whole and ground forms are used greatly in Indian cooking. When the whole seeds are added to hot oil (for baghar phoron) they emit a lovely aroma, before the vegetables or other spices are added.

Curry leaves (*Karipatta*) Used mainly in South Indian cooking, these have a distinctive flavor. In South India most people grow their own trees. The leaves can be found fresh or in dried form.

Fennel (*Sauf*) Light green, oval shaped seeds with a licorice flavor—used a great deal in Kashmiri cooking. As the seeds are a good digestive, they are sometimes dry roasted and served at the end of the meal.

Fenugreek (*Methi*) These seeds are yellow in color and have a bitter taste, so they are used in small amounts only. The seeds are used either whole or ground after dry roasting. In India, the leaves of the fenugreek plant are eaten as a vegetable.

Ginger (*Adrak*) The rhizome of a plant with a pungent flavor; it can be stored in the refrigerator for about one month. To use, peel the skin and use either grated or cut into strips. Ginger can be ground easily in an electric coffee grinder. Dry ginger powder is also available, but it loses its flavor if stored for too long.

Mango powder (*Amchoor*) This is made by peeling and slicing the unripe mango and drying it in the sun until it shrivels up. It is then powdered. Available at Indian grocery stores, it is added to a dish to make it sour.

Mustard (*Rye or sarson*) White and dark purple mustard seeds are available. In Indian cooking the darker variety is used. They are tiny and round in shape. When added to hot oil they start to splutter. At this stage, either the oil is poured over a cooked dish or vegetables are added to the oil. The seeds can be ground easily in an electric coffee grinder. The ground mustard is mixed with the hot water and covered and kept aside for 30 minutes to bring out the hotter taste of the mustard. In India the leaves of the mustard plant are eaten as a vegetable.

Onion seed (*Kalonji or kala jeera*) Small, black seeds used whole in vegetable and fish dishes in

Bengal. This is an important spice for pickling. In North India, onion seeds are sprinkled on some of the breads before baking.

Panch phoron A combination of five spices mixed in equal proportions: cumin, onion seed, fennel, fenugreek and mustard. Used for lentil or vegetable preparations and normally used whole.

Pistachio nuts (*Pista*) The kernel is green in color with a reddish brown skin, and the flavor is delicate. They are used as a garnish on desserts either chopped or slivered. To skin the pistachio nuts, place them in boiling water for 30 seconds and then immediately put them into cold water. The skin can then be removed easily. They are also available roasted and salted with the shell on.

Poppy seed (*Khuskhus*) Tiny, white, round seeds with a nutty taste, used in both sweet and salt dishes. Sometimes used as a thickening agent.

Saffron (*Kesar or zaffron*) These threads are orangey red in color and are the dried stems of a flower of the crocus family. In India they are grown mainly in Kashmir. A small amount of good quality saffron is enough to color and flavor a dish. It is usually soaked in warm milk and kept aside for 15–20 minutes before using.

Sesame (*Til*) Tiny, beige seeds with a nutty flavor. The sesame oil is used for cooking.

Tamarind (*Imli*) Tamarind trees grow in tropical climates. The pods are 5–7 in in length and become dark brown when ripe. The pulp is dried in the sun and sold in packets at Indian grocery stores. A little tamarind pulp is soaked in hot water for 30 minutes and then squeezed to drain out all the juice. It has a sour taste.

Turmeric (*Haldi*) Mainly found in ground form at Indian grocery stores or supermarkets. It is the root of a plant of the ginger family. Pungent in taste and yellow in color.

Oils

Many different kinds of oil are used for cooking in India. Some of the vegetable and fish dishes from Eastern India are normally cooked in mustard oil, but you can use vegetable oil.

Coconut oil (*Copra ka tel*) Has a delicate flavor and solidifies at low temperatures.

Groundnut oil (*Moongphali ka tel*) This is the oil from peanuts. It is used for cooking in Southern India and has a nutty flavor.

Mustard oil (*Sarson ka tel*) Yellow in color with a strong smell. Fish cooked in mustard oil has a distinctive flavor.

Sesame oil (*Til ka tel*) Has a strong, distinct flavour and is dark in color.
People from Kashmir, Bengal, Bihar and Uttar Pradesh use mustard oil. People from Gujarat and Tamil Nadu use sesame oil. People from Maharastra use peanut oil. People from Kerala use coconut oil.

Legumes (Dals)

There are many varieties available in India and a great many of these can be found in North America at Indian grocery stores. They are available whole or split.

Arhar dal Also called toor or toovar dal, this is the main dal used in Southern India.

Channa dal These are similar to split peas, but slightly smaller.

Chole (*Chickpeas or garbanzos*) Beige, round, dried peas. Should be soaked overnight to reduce the cooking time. Chickpea flour is called gram, and is widely used in cooking.

Lobia (*Black-eyed beans*) White, kidney-shaped beans with a black "eye". Popular in the North.

Masoor dal (*Split red lentils*) Salmon-coloured, small, flat, round lentils which cook easily.

Matar (*Split peas*) Round, yellow lentils which are uniform in size.

Moong dal Small, yellow, split lentils. Bean sprouts are made by sprouting these beans.

Rajma (*Red kidney beans*) Large, dark red kidney-shaped beans. Should be soaked overnight to reduce cooking time.

Toovar dal See Arhar dal

Urid dal (*Black gram*) The bean is reddish black in color, is very small in size and takes a long time to cook. The split urid dal is pale cream in color. It is usually soaked and ground to a paste as for Dahi vada, Dosa or Idli.

Left *Indian cuisine uses a wide variety of vegetables — some familiar and others more unusual. All are available fresh from Indian grocers'.*

1 *Pumpkin*   4 *White radish*
2 *Spinach*   5 *Okra*
3 *Doddy*   6 *Bitter gourd*

Moong dal

Masoor dal

Chole

Channa dal

Rajma

Urid dal

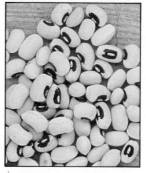
Lobia

Matar

SPECIAL TECHNIQUES

Adding spices to hot oil (*Baghar phoron*) Oil is heated until it is very hot, and whole spices, crushed garlic or green chilies are added until the spices swell up or splutter or change color. This is then added to a cooked dish, or vegetables, or other spices are added and cooking continues.

Dry roasting Place whole spices in a small, heavy based skillet and heat gently, stirring the spices constantly so that they do not burn. Soon the spices will turn a few shades darker and a lovely aroma will emerge.

Frying onions Place the oil in a skillet or saucepan over a medium high heat. When hot add the onions, and, stirring occasionally, fry until the onions start to change color. Lower the heat and continue to fry until they are reddish brown.

Adding yogurt while cooking When a recipe calls for yogurt, always whisk the yogurt until smooth, and add slowly, otherwise it curdles.

Peeling tomatoes Place the tomatoes in boiling water for 30 seconds. Drain and cool under running cold water. Peel, chop and use as required.

Cleaning chilies Pull out the stalks of the chilies and, holding them under cold running water, slit them open with a sharp knife and remove the seeds. The seeds are the hottest part of the chilies and most Indians do not remove them. Be very careful, when handling chilies, not to put your hands near your eyes as the oil will make your eyes burn.

Chilies can be stored for 12–14 days by removing the stalks of each chili and putting them in a closed bottle in the refrigerator. When needed, wash the chilies and use as required.

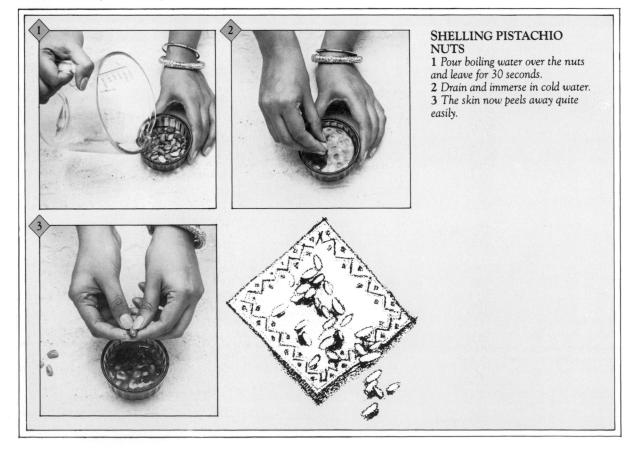

SHELLING PISTACHIO NUTS
1 *Pour boiling water over the nuts and leave for 30 seconds.*
2 *Drain and immerse in cold water.*
3 *The skin now peels away quite easily.*

CLEANING A CHILI

1 *Slice off the stalk end of the chili and hold it under cold running water. With a sharp knife, slit it open from top to bottom.*
2 *Remove all the seeds, keeping the chili under the running water to prevent the oil splashing into your eyes.*

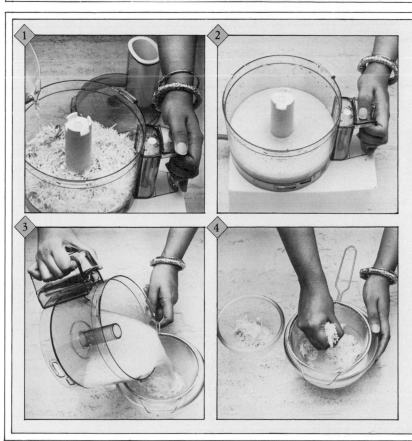

MAKING COCONUT MILK

1 *Add hot water to the grated coconut.*
2 *Blend the mixture until it is very smooth.*
3 *Pour through a sieve and collect the milk.*
4 *Squeeze the remaining milk out by hand.*

BASIC RECIPES

Panir

Home-made cottage cheese

MAKING PANIR
1 Bring the milk to the boil and slowly add the water and vinegar.
2 Stop adding vinegar as soon as the milk curdles.
3 Strain the curdled milk through several layers of cloth.
4 Tie the ends of the cloth and squeeze the liquid out.
5 Hang the cheese up to drain.

1 Bring the milk to a boil, stirring constantly, over a high heat. Remove from heat.

2 Combine the water and vinegar.

3 Slowly add the vinegar solution to the boiled milk, stirring with a wooden spoon. As soon as the milk curdles do not add any more. (The curd and whey will separate.)

4 Place three or four layers of cheesecloth in a sieve and strain the curdled milk through them. Tie up the ends of the cheesecloth and squeeze out as much of the liquid as possible. Hang it up to drain thoroughly.

When adding the water and vinegar mixture to the milk, do not add more than necessary as this tends to harden the panir.
Use in salt or sweet dishes.

15 cups milk
about 1 cup warm water
about 1/3 cup white vinegar
3 1/2 cups panir

Dahi

Yogurt

Yogurt is used a great deal in Indian cooking. It is used to marinate meats and to give flavor to certain types of curry.

As yogurt is very refreshing and cool it is eaten at most meals in certain parts of the country, particularly the North. It is eaten either plain or with some seasoning or vegetables added to it. In Bengal, sweetened yogurt is eaten as a dessert.

On a hot day it can be mixed with water to make a refreshing drink.

Most families in India make their own yogurt at home though it is easily available in the shops.

5 cups milk

2½ tbsp yogurt

1 Bring the milk to a boil, stirring constantly.

2 Remove from the heat and let it cool so that it feels just warm.

3 Place the yogurt in a large bowl and whisk until smooth. Slowly add the lukewarm milk and stir gently. Cover the bowl and leave in a warm place overnight. Chill and use as required.

Once you have made some yogurt you can keep a little aside for the next batch, if you are going to make it within a day or two.

Ghee

Clarified butter

Ghee can be bought at any Indian grocery store, but home-made ghee has a special flavor.

1 lb/2 cups unsalted butter

1 Heat the butter in a saucepan over a low heat. Let it simmer until all the white residue turns golden and settles at the bottom.

2 Remove from the heat, strain and cool.

3 Pour into an airtight bottle and store in a cool place.

Keeps for 1–2 months.

Imli Ki Rus

Tamarind juice

½ cup dried tamarind
1 cup hot water

1 Soak the tamarind in the water for about 30 minutes.

2 Squeeze the pulp well to draw out all the juice. Strain and use as required.

By altering the amount of water you can change the consistency.

Garam Masala

Mixed spice

3 tsp cardamom seeds
3 × 1 in pieces of stick cinnamon
1½ tsp cumin seeds
½ tsp black peppercorns
½ tsp cloves
¼ of a nutmeg

1 Grind all the spices together until they are finely ground.

2 Store in a spice bottle until required.

This is a combination of spices, and is used sparingly towards the end of the cooking time or sprinkled on right at the end.

The ingredients may be added in different proportions to suit individual taste.

Nariyal Ki Dudh

Coconut milk

When buying a coconut, shake it to make sure it is full of water. The more liquid it has, the fresher it is. (This liquid is not coconut milk, it is coconut water, and can be served as a drink when chilled.)

To open the coconut Take a screwdriver and punch two holes in the eyes of the coconut and drain off all the liquid. Place in a preheated oven at 375°F for 15–20 minutes. While the coconut is still hot, hit it with a hammer to split it and the flesh should come away from the shell.

To grate Peel off the brown skin from the coconut flesh and grate either with a hand grater or in a food processor.

To make coconut milk Combine the grated coconut with 2 cups of very hot water and blend. Pass this liquid through a sieve and squeeze the pulp to draw out all the liquid. This is known as thick coconut milk. The pulp is normally thrown away, but a few recipes may call for thin coconut milk, in which case the process is repeated using about 2 cups of hot water added to the coconut pulp. Blend the mixture and strain.

Thick milk has a lot more flavor than thin milk.

A quick method of making coconut milk is to blend together ½ cup creamed coconut with 2 scant cups of hot water. Creamed coconut is available in supermarkets in 7 oz slabs. It keeps in the refrigerator for 2–3 months.

Sukha Bhuna Jeera

Roasted cumin

2 tbsp whole cumin seeds

1 Place the cumin seeds in a small pan over a medium heat and dry roast them, stirring constantly. The seeds will then turn a few shades darker. (Take care not to burn them.)

2 Cool and grind finely. Store in a spice bottle until required.

Coriander seeds and dried red chilies can be roasted and ground in a similar manner and stored.

THE INDIAN KITCHEN

Indian food can be cooked easily in a modern kitchen and you do not need to go out to get a lot of equipment. However, you may be interested to know about some of the more traditional implements and utensils of the Indian kitchen.

A chula This is a hollow cube with a hole towards the bottom through which fuel is fed, and a hole at the top which acts as the burner. Midway there are four or five iron rods which act as a bracket to hold the coal. The chula must have mud placed regularly on the inside and outside, so that it does not lose its shape. The mud is then left to dry out. There is a special technique to placing the mud, to ensure that after it dries out there are no cracks. In the cities, gas or electric stoves are often used.

A degchi This is a pan without handles, made of polished brass, stainless steel or other metals. The lid of the degchi is slightly dipped so that sometimes live coal can be placed on it to cook food slowly or keep food warm. Ordinary saucepans with lids can be used in the same way and the oven can be used to cook food slowly or to keep it warm.

A karai This is found in every Indian kitchen. It is a deep, concave metallic dish with two handles —

one on each side. It looks like a Chinese wok but it is a little more rounded. It is used for deep frying, as it uses less oil than a deep fryer; and for the same reason, I also use it to cook vegetables and fish. A deep fryer or saucepan or skillet can be used if you do not have a karai.

A tava This is made from cast iron, is slightly concave, and is about 10 in in diameter. It is ideal for making chappatis or parathas because it distributes the heat evenly. A griddle or heavy skillet will serve the same purpose.

Tongs These are used to remove a karai from the fire, or to remove the hot lid from the degchi. To remove the degchi from the fire it is normally held at either side with a cloth.

Metallic stirrers These are used in India because the pans are not non stick. Use wooden spoons when using non stick pans. Wooden spoons are easier to use as they do not get hot, although if left in hot oil they tend to burn.

A thick stone slab This is used with a round stone roller like a rolling pin for grinding. Whole spices are ground with a little water; if dry ground spice is required a mortar and pestle is used. Lentils are also ground on the slab.

Right *Modern kitchen equipment, such as a food processor, garlic press and stainless steel knives, can be put to good use in the preparation of many Indian dishes.*

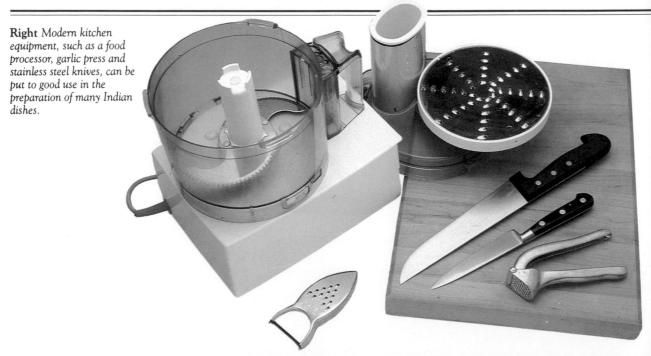

Below *The tandoor or clay oven is used widely in the northern regions. Tandoori* *meats are marinated and then dry-cooked at speed in the intense heat of the tandoor.*

A tandoor This is a clay oven used in Northern India. Tandoori chicken, whole or in pieces, different kinds of breads and kebobs are baked in this oven. It is about 3–4 ft deep and about 2 ft wide on top with a hole of 12 in diameter through which the food is put for cooking. It is fuelled by wood and coal and intensive heat builds up inside. This oven, too, has mud patted on the inside and outside and it must be allowed to dry out. The chicken or the kebobs are marinated and then skewered and placed in the tandoor; the intensity of the heat cooks a whole chicken in a matter of minutes.

When bread is baked in a tandoor, the dough is slapped onto the inside of the oven and when bubbles form, which is in a matter of a few seconds, the bread is cooked. It does not need to be turned over.

Tandoori chicken can be cooked easily in the modern oven, and then put under a very hot broiler for a few minutes to dry out. It can also taste excellent barbecued.

An electric coffee grinder In the modern kitchen, this can be used to grind spices. A blender or food processor may be used to blend onions, lentils and rice. The food processor can be used to make the dough for most of the breads and to save time when grating vegetables.

Right *Traditional kitchen equipment includes the karai, shown on the left of the picture with tongs to lift it from the heat and a wooden stirrer. The heavy skillet and saucepan on the right of the picture are suitable modern substitutes for the tava and the degchi.*

NORTHERN INDIA

The region of Northern India is rich in geographical, cultural and culinary tradition. It embraces Kashmir, the jewel of the north, Simla, the summer capital of the British Raj, the Punjab, with its famed tandoori cooking and the cosmopolitan city of Delhi, with its many different types of cuisine.

Northern India could be said to have the most beautiful scenery in the country, and Kashmir is the jewel of the North. Kashmir is a large valley in the Himalayan mountains and its people are mainly Muslims. Both Hindus and Muslims in Kashmir are non-vegetarian; even the Brahmins of this state eat meat. Interestingly, though, the Brahmins exclude garlic and onions from their diet as these are said to make the body hot. They use a lot of fennel and yogurt in their cooking, both known to be refreshing, and a great deal of saffron, which grows in the area. Used to flavor and color a dish, saffron is the dried stem of the flower of the crocus family.

If you were to visit a Kashmiri Muslim's home, you would find that the women eat in separate rooms from the men. Mats would be laid on the floor for you to sit on, and a large thali, filled with a selection of delicacies, would be placed in the middle of the room; everyone would eat from there. Kashmiris eat a lot of rice and meat; they are not allowed alcohol but drink plenty of spiced tea.

However, a proper "Persian dinner", given on state occasions by Kashmiri Muslims, is a very different affair. Officially, there should be 36 courses, but, mercifully, these are usually reduced to 18; even so the diners find themselves struggling towards the end, grateful for the little bowls of cinnamon tea that mark the end of the meal. The pilafs are spectacular. The favorite meat of the Prophet was camel, and, during his reign, it was quite common to see a solitary beast being walked to the palace during Ramadan for the feast of Id.

The Dal Lake at Srinagar is one of Kashmir's main attractions. It is famed for its houseboats, which people can rent for specified periods. Each has its own cook and operates like a rented villa, floating on water. North east from Kashmir lies Ladakh, only recently opened to tourists; people there are mainly of the Buddhist faith and their culture is strongly Tibetan.

The cooking styles of Northern India show traces of Moghul influence dating from the eighth century when the Moghuls first invaded the country. There is a variety of lamb dishes: kebobs, either broiled or fried, and curries, which can be served dry or with gravy. Lamb became very important in the region, as the Moghuls, being Muslim, would not eat pork, and the Hindus would not eat beef because they considered the cow to be sacred.

Moghlai food is also cooked by the Muslims of Lucknow in Uttar Pradesh—who are famous for their kebobs—and by the Muslims of Hyderabad in Andhra Pradesh. It is for this reason that I have given the recipe for Biriyani (Rice with lamb) in the Southern section (*see Hyderabadi Biriyani*). A famous Moghlai dish in the North is Murgh masallam (Spicy roast chicken)—a whole stuffed roast chicken that has been marinated in spices and yogurt.

During their rule, the Moghuls built fine buildings of some architectural importance, whereas the Hindus were noted for their proficiency in music, art, literature and dance. Simla, the capital of Himachal Pradesh, was the old summer capital in the days of the British Raj. Discovered by the British in 1819, women retreated there for the summer and their menfolk joined them when their duties permitted. Situated at an altitude of 830 ft, it offered, and still offers, welcome mountain air during the stifling summer months. For about 100 years, Indians were not allowed to visit Simla. Summer retreats such as this were commonly known as hill stations.

The Kulu valley in this state has the Beas River running through it, and the impressive, snow capped Himalayas provide the background. The valley is rich with innumerable lakes, and fishing is plentiful although this is for sport only and not for food. The local people are good spinners and weavers, and make wonderful shawls from the fleece of the mountain goat. The men wear the distinctive Kulu cap, a pillbox-shaped hat with a flap at the back, and the women wear long, homespun garments and lots of silver jewellery.

The cuisines of Himachal Pradesh, Punjab and Haryana are similar. This is because before the partition of India and Pakistan the area was one large state, known as the Punjab; now the border

between the two countries cuts through the area. The people of Punjab are either Sikhs or Hindus: the Sikhs now live in the state of Punjab and the Hindu Punjabis live in Haryana. Punjabi food is particularly noteworthy. As this is an agricultural state, their food is not as rich as Moghlai food, and Tandoori cooking has become a speciality. Much rice and wheat is grown here, and rotis (breads) are popular. There are many varieties of breads, including chappati, poori, paratha, a whole range of stuffed paratha, tandoori roti (*see entry for a tandoor in Introduction*) and naan. Paratha stuffed with vegetables is best eaten with hot pickles and yogurt (*see Breads and Rice, and Accompaniments for recipes*). Famous Punjabi vegetarian dishes are Sarson ki saag (Mustard greens), Makki ki roti (Corn flour bread—*see Breads and Rice for recipe*), and Mahan ki dal (Whole black beans). Kulfi (Indian style ice cream) made with plenty of nuts is a delicious and refreshing way to end a meal. When carrots are in season the Punjabis make full use of them in pickles, salads and as a dessert in the dish Gajjar halva (Carrot halva). Punjabi Sikhs make a practice of distributing food in their gurdwaras, or temples, to any needy person of any faith.

Delhi has been the capital of India since the early twentieth century. It is divided into two sections: Old Delhi and New Delhi. In Old Delhi, much Moghul architecture still exists, such as the Red Fort, and the mosques and tombs; the roads are very narrow and the markets dingy. New Delhi was built earlier this century and has a completely different flavor, with wide roads and newer buildings. Politically, Delhi is the heart of the country and has attracted a comparatively cosmopolitan population. Consequently it boasts many different types of cuisine.

The climate in the northern part of India fluctuates wildly during the year—very hot summers and very cold winters are the norm. However, you can escape the heat, and summers in Simla and Kashmir are usually pleasant.

Kabli Channa

Spicy chickpeas (garbanzos)

LEGUMES

1 Soak the chickpeas overnight in the measured amount of water.

2 Boil the chickpeas in the same water, cover and simmer for about 1 hour until tender. Drain and save the liquid.

3 Heat the oil in a large saucepan over a medium high heat and add the asafetida and cumin seeds. Let them sizzle for a few seconds.

4 Add the drained chickpeas, turmeric, chili powder, coriander, cumin, mango powder and salt and stir fry for 2–3 minutes.

5 Add 1 cup of the chickpea broth and cook for 20 minutes, stirring occasionally.

6 Before serving, pour on the lemon juice and sprinkle with the coriander leaves and green chilies.

Serve with Batora.

1 scant cup chickpeas, washed
3¾ cups water
4 tbsp oil
pinch of asafetida
½ tsp whole cumin seeds
½ tsp ground turmeric
½ tsp chili powder
1 tsp ground coriander
1 tsp ground cumin
1½ tsp mango powder
½ tsp salt
2 tbsp lemon juice
1 tbsp coriander leaves, chopped
1–2 green chilies, chopped

Rajma

Spicy red kidney beans

LEGUMES

1 Soak the beans in the water overnight.

2 Bring the beans to a boil in the same water, cover and simmer for about 1 hour until tender. Drain.

3 Heat the oil in a large saucepan over a medium high heat; add the cinnamon, cardamom and cloves and let them sizzle for a few seconds.

4 Add the onion, garlic and ginger and, stirring occasionally, fry until the onion is golden brown.

5 Add the turmeric, chili, salt and tomatoes and fry for 1 minute.

1 scant cup red kidney beans, washed
5 cups water
6 tbsp oil
2 in piece of stick cinnamon
3 cardamom pods
3 cloves
1 large onion, finely sliced
2 cloves garlic, crushed
½ in ginger, grated
¾ tsp ground turmeric
½ tsp chili powder
½ tsp salt
2 tomatoes, chopped
½ cup water
2 bay leaves

6 Add the drained beans, mix with the spices and fry for another 2–3 minutes.

7 Add ½ cup water and bring to a boil, cover, lower heat and cook for 15–20 minutes until the spices are well blended with the beans.

Garnish with bay leaves and serve with chappatis.

Mahan Ki Dal

Whole black beans

1 Wash the beans in several changes of water.

2 Place the beans, ginger, chilies, garlic, salt and water in a large saucepan and bring to a boil. Lower the heat, cover, leaving the lid slightly ajar, and simmer for about 3–3½ hours until the beans are soft. (Add more water if required.)

3 Mash the beans slightly and add the yogurt and 1 tbsp of the ghee. Cook for a further 30 minutes. (When the beans are cooked they should turn reddish brown in color and the consistency should be thick.)

4 Heat the remaining ghee and fry the onion until lightly golden. Add this to the hot beans and garnish with the coriander leaves.

The beans could also be boiled in a pressure cooker at 15 lb weight for 15–20 minutes.

LEGUMES

¾ cup whole black beans (sabut urid)
½ in ginger, grated
3 dried red chilies
4 cloves garlic, crushed
1½ tsp salt
6–7½ cups water
3 tbsp yogurt, lightly beaten
4 tbsp ghee
1 small onion, chopped
1 tbsp coriander leaves, chopped

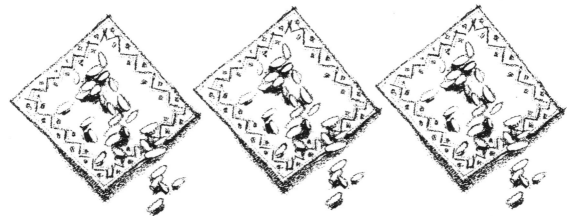

◇ **Kabli channa**/Spicy chickpeas — *see page 28*

Aloo Methi

Potatoes with fenugreek leaves

VEGETABLES

1 lb potatoes
½ cup fresh fenugreek leaves
or
1 tbsp dried fenugreek leaves
3 tbsp ghee
½ tsp ground turmeric
1 tsp ground cumin
½ tsp chili powder
1 tsp salt

1 Wash the potatoes and then peel and cut them into ¾ in cubes.

2 If you are using fresh fenugreek, remove the tough lower stalk, wash the leaves thoroughly and chop finely. If you are using dried fenugreek, soak it in water for about 20–25 minutes, gently squeeze the water out and chop the leaves. Remove any tough stalks.

3 Heat the ghee in a large skillet. Add the potatoes and, stirring constantly, fry for about 3–4 minutes.

4 Add the turmeric, cumin, chili and salt and mix with the potatoes and cook for a further minute.

5 Add the fenugreek leaves and mix with the potatoes. Lower the heat, cover and, stirring occasionally, cook for about 20 minutes until the potatoes are tender. Add 1–2 tbsp of water if necessary.

⬦ **Aloo methi**/Potatoes with fenugreek leaves — *see page 30*

Baigan Bharta

Spicy eggplant

VEGETABLES

1 lb eggplant, split lengthwise
3 tbsp oil
1 large onion, finely chopped
3 tomatoes, chopped
1 tbsp coriander leaves, chopped
1–2 green chilies, chopped
½ tsp ground turmeric
½ tsp chili powder
¾ tsp ground coriander
¾ tsp salt

1 Place the eggplant under a preheated broiler for about 15 minutes, turning the halves frequently until the skin becomes black and the flesh soft. Carefully peel off the skin and mash the flesh.

2 Heat the oil in a karai or saucepan over a medium heat and fry the onion until soft. Add the tomatoes, coriander leaves and green chilies and fry for another 2–3 minutes.

3 Add the eggplant flesh, turmeric, chili, coriander and salt and mix thoroughly.

4 Fry for another 10–12 minutes and serve hot with chappatis.

Pakoras

Vegetable fritters

VEGETABLES

Batter
4 tbsp gram flour
2 tsp oil
1 tsp baking powder
½ tsp salt
about ⅓ cup water
Any of the following vegetables can be used
eggplant: cut into very thin rounds
onion: cut into ⅛ in rings
potato: cut into very thin rounds
cauliflower: cut into ¾ in florets
chili: leave whole
pumpkin: cut into thin slices
green pepper or capsicum: cut into thin strips
You can use a few slices of 3 – 4 different vegetables or one type only.
oil for deep frying

1 Mix all the batter ingredients together to make a smooth paste.

2 Wash the slices of vegetables and pat dry.

3 Heat the oil in a karai or saucepan until very hot.

4 Dip a slice of a vegetable in the batter and put into the hot oil. Place as many slices as you can into the oil. Fry until crisp and golden. Drain and serve with mint or coriander chutney.

Matar Panir

Cheese with peas

1 Cut the panir into ½ in cubes.

2 Blend the onion, garlic, ginger and tomatoes to a purée.

3 Heat the oil in a karai or saucepan over a medium high heat and fry the panir cubes, a few at a time, turning frequently, until golden brown. Remove and drain on paper towels and put to one side.

4 In the remaining oil add the blended mixture and fry for 3–4 minutes, stirring constantly, until the oil comes to the top.

5 Add the turmeric, chili, coriander and salt and continue to fry for another 1–2 minutes.

6 Add the peas and stir to mix with the spices. Add the water and bring to a boil. Cover, lower heat to medium low and simmer for 5 minutes. Add the fried panir and simmer for a further 10 minutes. Garnish with the coriander leaves.

1⅔ cups panir, drained
1 medium onion, quartered
2 cloves garlic
½ in ginger
2 tomatoes
6 tbsp oil
1 tsp ground turmeric
½ tsp chili powder
1 tsp ground coriander
1 tsp salt
¾ cup peas (fresh or frozen)
1 cup water
1 tbsp coriander leaves, chopped

Matar Gobi

Peas and cauliflower with ginger

1 Heat the oil in a karai or saucepan over a medium high heat. Add the ginger and fry, stirring constantly, until slightly browned.

2 Add the cauliflower, peas, turmeric and salt and mix with the ginger.

3 Lower heat, cover and, stirring occasionally, cook for about 20–25 minutes until the vegetables are tender.

4 Garnish with the coriander leaves.

3 tbsp oil
½ cup ginger, cut into very thin strips
1 small cauliflower, broken into large florets
1½ cups peas
1 tsp ground turmeric
1 tsp salt
2 tbsp coriander leaves, chopped

◆ **Pakoras**/Vegetable fritters
   (above) — see page 32

◆ **Matar panir**/Cheese with peas
   (below) — see page 33

◆ **Baigan bharta**/Spicy eggplant
— *see page 32*

Sarson Ki Saag

Spicy mustard leaves

VEGETABLES

1 lb/2 cups mustard leaves	
½ lb/1 cup spinach	
2–3 green chilies, chopped	
1 tsp salt	
½ cup water	
about 2 tbsp corn flour	
2 tbsp ghee	
1 onion, finely chopped	
½ in ginger, grated	
4 cloves garlic, crushed	
4 tbsp butter	

1 Wash the greens and chop finely.

2 Place the greens, chilies, salt and water in a large saucepan and cook on a low heat, stirring occasionally. A lot of water is given out by the greens, but if all the moisture dries up before the greens are cooked, add a little more water. Cook until the greens are tender and all the moisture has evaporated.

3 Place this mixture in a food processor or liquidizer and blend to a purée without adding any more water.

4 After blending, add enough corn flour and mix into the purée to the desired consistency.

5 Heat the ghee in a large skillet, add the onion, ginger and garlic and fry until lightly golden.

6 Add the puréed greens and, stirring constantly, cook for about 3–4 minutes over a medium heat.

7 Put in a serving dish with the butter on top.

Serve with Makki ki roti.

Sukha Aloo

VEGETABLES

Dry potatoes

1 Heat the ghee in a karai or saucepan over a medium high heat. Add the cumin seeds and let them sizzle for 5–6 seconds.

2 Add the potatoes and continue to fry until lightly browned.

3 Add the salt and pepper and continue to cook for a further 2–3 minutes.

1½ lb/6 cups potatoes, boiled and diced into ½ in cubes
2 tbsp ghee
2 tsp cumin seeds
1 tsp salt
½ tsp ground black pepper

Sukha Matar

VEGETABLES

Dry peas

1 Heat the oil in a karai or saucepan over a medium high heat and fry the ginger, stirring constantly, until slightly browned.

2 Add the peas and salt and mix with the ginger.

3 Lower the heat, cover and cook for about 15 minutes until the peas are tender.

4 Add the mango powder, mix and remove from the heat.

2 tbsp oil
2 in ginger, cut into very thin strips
1½ lb/3 cups peas (fresh or frozen)
1 tsp salt
½ tsp mango powder

Fresh emerald-green chilies contrast strikingly with plump, purple eggplants.

◆ **Sukha matar**/Dry peas *(top)* — *see page 37*   ◆ **Sukha aloo**/Dry potatoes *(above)* — *see page 37*

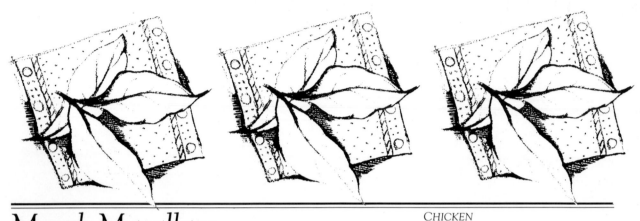

Murgh Masallam

CHICKEN

Spicy roast chicken

3½ lb chicken, cleaned

Stuffing

1 Heat the oil in a pan over a medium high heat. Fry the onion until lightly golden.

2 Add all the remaining ingredients and fry for another 2–3 minutes.

3 Stuff the body cavity of the chicken.

Stuffing
1 tbsp oil
⅓ cup onion, finely chopped
1 large potato, boiled and diced
2 eggs, boiled and chopped
¼ cup peas, boiled
½ tsp salt
¼ tsp pepper
1–2 green chilies, chopped
1 tbsp coriander leaves, chopped
1½ tbsp ground almonds

Marinade

1 Blend together all the ingredients except the oil.

2 Stir the oil into the blended mixture.

3 Rub the chicken all over with the marinade and set aside for 5–6 hours.

4 Place in a preheated oven at 425°F for 20 minutes. Cover with foil, lower heat to 375°F and bake for a further 1½ hours. Remove the cover for the last 30 minutes of the cooking time.

To serve, place the chicken on a platter and offer the sauce separately in a bowl.

Marinade
⅔ cup onions, cut up
2–3 cloves garlic
1 in ginger
½ tsp ground turmeric
½ tsp chili powder
¾ tsp garam masala powder
2 tbsp blanched almonds
½ cup yogurt
1 tsp salt
4 tbsp oil

Tandoori Murgh

Tandoori chicken

CHICKEN

2½ lb chicken
1 tsp coriander seeds
1 tsp cumin seeds
1 in ginger, grated
4 cloves garlic, crushed
1½ tsp salt
1 tsp chili powder
1 cup yogurt
few drops red food coloring (optional)
ghee for basting
juice of ½ a lemon

1 Skin the chicken and cut into 8 pieces. With a sharp knife make 2 or 3 slits in each piece of chicken.

2 Dry roast the coriander and cumin seeds, stirring constantly, until they turn a few shades darker. Grind to a fine powder.

3 Mix together the coriander and cumin powder with the ginger, garlic, salt, chili powder, yogurt and coloring.

4 Place the chicken pieces in a large bowl and pour the yogurt mixture on top, coating the chicken pieces thoroughly. Cover and marinate overnight.

5 Place the chicken pieces and the marinade on a baking sheet and place in a preheated oven at 375°F for about 1 hour, basting with the ghee and marinade occasionally, and turning the pieces so that they become evenly browned.

6 Place the chicken pieces without the juices under a very hot broiler for 5–7 minutes each side so that they become dry. Squeeze the lemon juice on top before serving.

Murgh Pakora

Fried chicken

CHICKEN

1 medium size chicken, skinned and cut into 8 pieces
1 cup plain flour
1 egg
4 cloves garlic, crushed
¾ in ginger, grated
1 cup yogurt
1 dried red chili, roasted and ground
¼ tsp garam masala powder
1 tsp salt
½ tsp pepper
few drops red food coloring
¾ tsp roasted cumin seeds, ground
oil for deep frying

1 Wash the pieces of chicken and pat dry. Make 2–3 slits in each piece.

2 Mix all the other ingredients together and make sure all the pieces are fully coated. Marinate for about 6 hours.

3 Deep fry over a medium heat for 12–15 minutes until nicely golden and cooked right through.

Serve sprinkled with Chaat masala.

◆ **Tandoori murgh**/Tandoori chicken (top) from the
Punjab — see page 41. Fresh garlic (above) is an
essential ingredient in Indian cuisine

◆ **Murgh massallam**/Spicy roast chicken *(top)*, a famous Moghlai dish — *see page 40*

◆ **Murgh pakora**/Fried chicken *(above)* — *see page 41*

Machi Pakora

FISH

Fried fish

1 Cut the fish into 2 in wide pieces. Wash and pat dry.

2 Mix the garlic, ginger, poppy seeds, garam masala, mustard and chili thoroughly.

3 Make a smooth, thick batter with the flour, gram flour and yogurt. Add the spices and salt.

4 Add the pieces of fish and coat well with the batter. Put to one side for 3–4 hours.

5 Heat oil over a medium high heat and fry the fish for about 8 minutes, until golden.

1 lb fillets of fish
2 cloves garlic, crushed
½ in ginger, grated
1 tsp poppy seeds, roasted and ground
½ tsp garam masala powder
1 tsp ground mustard
½ tsp chili powder
½ cup plain flour
½ cup gram flour
1 cup yogurt
1 tsp salt
oil for deep frying

Bara Kabab

MEAT

Lamb chop kebabs

1 Remove excess fat from the chops. Wash and pat dry.

2 Lightly beat the yogurt and mix in all the ingredients.

3 Add the lamb chops and marinate for at least 6 hours. (I usually like to marinate for 24 hours—if you are going to marinate for this long, cover and refrigerate the meat but make sure it is returned to room temperature before it is grilled or broiled.)

4 Preheat the grill or broiler.

5 Take the chops out of the marinade and place on a baking sheet. Grill or broil for 8–10 minutes on each side.

Serve with onion salad.

1½ lb lamb chops
2 cups yogurt
1½ tsp salt
1 in ginger, grated
8 cloves garlic, crushed
¾ tsp garam masala powder
1 tbsp poppy seeds, ground
2–3 green chilies, ground
2 tbsp oil

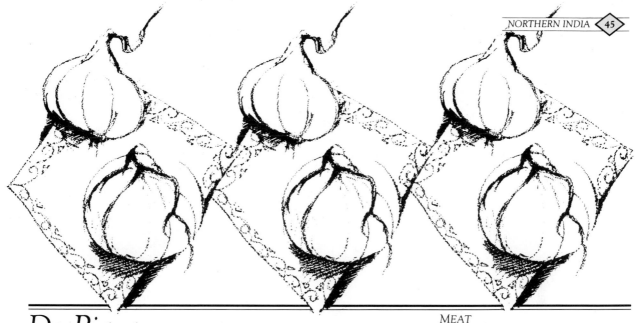

Do Piaza

MEAT

Lamb with onions

1 Marinate the lamb with the turmeric, chili, cumin, coriander, ginger, garlic, yogurt and salt and set aside for 3–4 hours.

2 Cut three of the onions in half and finely slice them. Chop the remaining onion.

3 Heat the oil in a large saucepan over a medium high heat and fry the sliced onions, stirring occasionally, until golden brown. Drain on paper towels and put aside.

4 In the remaining oil add the cardamom, cinnamon and cloves and let them sizzle for 4–5 seconds.

5 Add the chopped onion and fry until lightly browned. Add the meat and spices and fry, stirring constantly, for about 5–7 minutes.

6 Cover, lower heat to very low and simmer for about 1 hour until tender.

7 Add two thirds of the fried onions and mix with the meat and cook for another minute.

8 Garnish with the remaining onions.

2 lb/5⅓ cups lamb, cut into 1 in cubes
½ tsp ground turmeric
½ tsp chili powder
1 tsp ground cumin seeds
1 tsp ground coriander seeds
1 in ginger, grated
2 cloves garlic, crushed
1½ cups yogurt
1 tsp salt
4 large onions
10 tbsp oil
4 cardamom pods
2 in piece of stick cinnamon
3 cloves

◆ **Bara kabab**/Lamb chop kebobs — *see page 44*

◆ Sacks of garlic, grains,
powdered ginger and red
chili arrayed on an Indian
market stall

◆ **Do Piaza**/Lamb with onions — *see page 45*

MEAT

Kofta Curry

Meatball curry

1 Place all the kofta ingredients, except the eggs, in the food processor and blend until well mixed. Add the eggs and mix in thoroughly.

2 Using your hands, divide the mixture into 12–14 portions and form into balls between the palms of your hands. Put to one side.

3 Heat the oil in a large saucepan over a medium high heat and fry the onion until brown.

4 Add the turmeric, chili, coriander, cumin and salt and fry for about 30 seconds.

5 Add the tomatoes, mix with the spices and cook until soft. Add the water and bring to a boil.

6 Add the meatballs gently and boil rapidly for 10 minutes.

7 Lower the heat, cover and cook for 15 minutes, turning the koftas gently every 5–6 minutes. Add the yogurt, stir gently, cover again and cook for a further 15–20 minutes until all the water has been absorbed and a thick, rich gravy remains. Garnish with the coriander leaves.

Kofta

1½ lb/3 cups lamb, ground
1 large onion
¾ in ginger
8 cloves garlic
2 tsp poppy seeds, ground
¾ tsp ground coriander
¾ tsp ground cumin
2–3 green chilies
1 tsp salt
2 eggs, lightly beaten

Curry

6 tbsp oil
1 large onion, finely chopped
¾ tsp ground turmeric
½ tsp chili powder
1 tsp ground coriander
1 tsp ground cumin
1 tsp salt
3 tomatoes, chopped
1½ cups water
¾ cup yogurt
2–3 tbsp coriander leaves, chopped

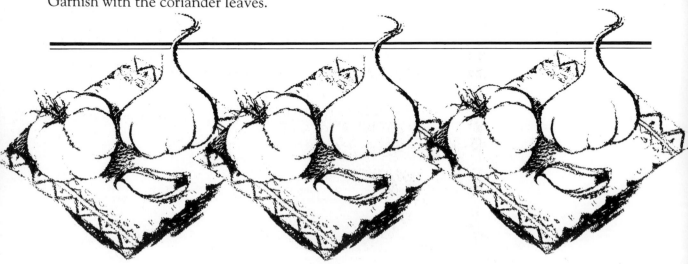

Kashmiri Rogan Josh

MEAT

Kashmiri lamb with fennel seeds

1 Place the fennel seeds in a grinder and grind until fine.

2 Heat oil in a large saucepan over a high heat. Add the asafetida and after 2 seconds add the cinnamon, cardamom and cloves and let them sizzle for 4–5 seconds.

3 Add the lamb and fry, stirring constantly, for about 5–7 minutes. Add the paprika, chili, ginger and salt and fry for another 2–3 minutes.

4 Add the yogurt, mix with the lamb, and cook for 10 minutes. Add the fennel, stir well to mix, cover, lower heat to very low and cook for about 1 hour, stirring occasionally, until the meat is tender and the gravy thickened.

Serve with rice.

1¾ tsp whole fennel seeds
6 tbsp oil
good pinch of asafetida
2 in piece of stick cinnamon
4 cardamom pods
4 cloves
2 lb/5⅓ cups lamb, cut into 1 in cubes
2 tsp paprika
2 tsp chili powder
1½ tsp ground ginger
1 tsp salt
2¼ cups yogurt, lightly beaten

Nargis Kofta

MEAT

Hard cooked eggs wrapped in spicy meat

1 Mix the ground meat well with the coriander, salt, chilies, garlic, onion, lemon juice and the beaten egg.

2 Divide into 4 portions.

3 Take 1 portion and wrap it around a hard cooked egg, making sure no holes appear.

4 Deep fry over a medium high heat for about 4–5 minutes until nicely browned.

5 Cut in half lengthwise to serve.

¾ lb/1½ cups finely ground lamb
2 tbsp coriander leaves, finely chopped
1 tsp salt
2–3 green chilies, finely chopped
3 cloves garlic, crushed
3 tbsp onions, finely chopped
3 tbsp lemon juice
1 egg, beaten
4 hard cooked eggs
oil for deep frying

◆ **Nargis kofta**/Hard cooked eggs wrapped in spicy ground lamb — *see page 49*

Saag Gosht

Meat with spinach

MEAT

1 Heat the oil in a large saucepan, add the cardamom, cinnamon and bay leaves and let them sizzle for 4–5 seconds.

2 Add the onions, garlic and ginger and fry until the onions are golden brown; add the turmeric and chili and fry for another minute.

3 Add the lamb and salt and mix well with the spices.

4 Cover, lower heat to very low and cook for about 30 minutes, stirring occasionally.

5 Add the spinach and continue to cook until all the liquid has evaporated.

Serve with Pilaf or Paratha.

6 tbsp oil
4 cardamom pods
2 in piece of stick cinnamon
3 bay leaves
2 medium onions, finely sliced
2 cloves garlic, crushed
¾ in ginger, grated
½ tsp ground turmeric
1 tsp chili powder
1½ lb/4 cups lamb, cut into 1 in cubes
1 tsp salt
1½ lb frozen spinach, chopped

Shahi Korma

MEAT

Lamb with almonds and yogurt

2 lb onions	
2 lb/5⅓ cups lamb, cut into 1 in cubes	
1 tsp ground coriander	
1 tsp ground cumin	
1 tsp chili powder	
1½ tsp salt	
1 cup oil	
2 cups yogurt	
½ tsp garam masala, ground	
2 tsp poppy seeds, ground	
7 cloves garlic, crushed	
1 in ginger, grated	
6 cardamom pods, slightly crushed	
½ cup almonds, blanched and slivered	
1 cup light cream	

1 Peel all the onions and finely chop half of them. Finely slice the other half.

2 Put the lamb in a large bowl, add the chopped onions, coriander, cumin, chili and salt, mix with the meat and marinate for 4–5 hours.

3 Heat the oil in a large skillet and fry the sliced onions until brown. Drain them on paper towels and blend to a fine paste in a liquidizer or food processor without adding any water. (Keep the oil for making the curry.)

4 Place the yogurt, garam masala and poppy seeds in a bowl, add the onion paste, mix thoroughly and put aside.

5 Heat 6 tbsp of the oil in a large saucepan over a medium high heat; add the garlic and ginger and fry until very lightly golden.

6 Add the lamb and the spices and mix with the oil. Lower the heat and, stirring occasionally, cook until all the water that came out of the lamb has been absorbed.

7 Add the yogurt paste, cardamom and almonds and mix with the meat. Cover and cook for about 30 minutes until the lamb is tender and the gravy very thick.

8 Add the cream and stir gently to mix. Cook for a further 10 minutes.

After the gravy has thickened and the lamb is tender, it can be put in an ovenproof dish, the cream gently mixed in and then placed in a preheated oven at 350°F for 10 minutes.

Serve with Pilaf.

Makki Ki Roti

BREAD

Corn starch bread

1 Sieve the flour and salt together.

2 Add enough water to make a stiff dough. Knead with your palms for about 10 minutes until soft and smooth.

3 Divide the dough into 8–10 balls.

4 Take one of the balls and place it on a lightly floured surface and, with the palm of your hand, press the ball gently to about 5 in diameter and less than ¼ in thick. (If the dough tends to stick to your hand place a little flour on top of the dough.)

5 Gently lift out the roti and place on a hot tava or skillet and cook until lightly golden. Turn and cook the other side in the same way.

6 Pierce the roti a few times with a fork, and brush with the melted butter. Do all the rotis in the same way.

Serve with Sarson ki saag.

2½ cups coarse cornstarch
pinch of salt
about ½ cup hot water
melted butter

Kheer

DESSERT

Creamed rice

1 Wash the rice in several changes of water and soak in plenty of water for 30 minutes. Drain.

2 Bring the milk to a boil over a high heat, stirring constantly. Lower the heat and simmer for 30 minutes, stirring occasionally.

3 Add the drained rice and sugar and continue to cook for a further 30–40 minutes until the milk has thickened and the rice is very soft and disintegrated.

4 Add the almonds and continue to cook for a further 10 minutes, stirring constantly.

2 tbsp basmati rice
5 cups milk
⅓ cup sugar
2 tbsp peeled almonds
¼ tsp ground cardamom
1 tsp rose water

5 Remove from the heat and stir in the cardamom and rose water.

6 Place in a serving dish and refrigerate.

Serve chilled.

Kulfi

Ice cream with almonds and pistachio nuts

5 cups milk
3½ tbsp sugar
2 tbsp ground almonds
2 tbsp pistachio nuts, skinned and chopped
few drops rose water

In India, Kulfi is usually frozen in individual, conical shaped metal containers with lids. To break up the ice crystals during freezing, instead of stirring the mixture, the containers are gently rolled between the palms of your hands. To serve, they are once again rolled between the palms, removed from the containers and cut into thick slices.

Kulfi can be made easily in any kind of container that can be placed in the freezer.

1 Bring the milk to a boil, stirring constantly.

2 Lower the heat and simmer, stirring occasionally, until it reduces to about 2 cups.

3 Add the sugar and mix thoroughly. Continue to simmer for another 2–3 minutes. Remove from the heat and let it cool completely.

4 Add the almonds and mix into the thickened milk, making sure no lumps form.

5 Stir in the pistachio nuts and rose water.

6 Place the mixture in a dish, cover it with its own lid or aluminum foil and place it in the freezer.

7 Take it out of the freezer after 20 minutes and give it a good stir to break up the ice crystals. Repeat twice more.

8 After this, it may be divided up into six chilled individual dishes, and covered and frozen for about 4–5 hours. Take it out of the freezer about 10 minutes before you are ready to serve.

Gajjar Halva

Carrot halva

1 Place the carrots, milk, sugar and cardamom in a large saucepan and bring to a boil. Lower heat to medium low and, stirring occasionally, cook until all the liquid has evaporated.

2 Heat the ghee in a large skillet over a medium heat, add the cooked carrots, raisins and pistachio and, stirring constantly, fry for 15–20 minutes until the mixture is dry and has turned reddish in color.

Serve hot or cold.

1 lb/4 cups carrots, peeled and grated
3¾ cups milk
⅔ cup sugar
3 cardamom pods
4 tbsp ghee
2 tbsp raisins
2 tbsp pistachio nuts, skinned and chopped

Sooji Halva

1 Boil the sugar and water over a medium heat for about 5 minutes to make a thin syrup. Put to one side.

2 Heat the ghee in a large saucepan over a medium heat. Add the semolina and, stirring constantly, fry until lightly golden.

3 Add the syrup and continue to stir until it leaves the sides of the saucepan and forms a ball.

4 Sprinkle on the cardamom seeds, almonds and the rose water.

½ cup sugar
2 cups water
4 tbsp ghee
1 cup semolina
6 cardamom pods, shelled
3 tbsp blanched almonds, slivered
few drops rose water (optional)

TYPICAL MENUS

Naan
Tandoori murgh
Matar pillau
Sukha aloo
Shahi korma
Raita
Kheer
★ ★ ★
Chappati
Mahan ki dal
Sukha matar
Baigan bharta
Saag gosht
Sooji halva

◆ **Kheer**/Creamed rice *(top)* — *see page 52*　　◆ **Gajjar halva**/Carrot halva *(above)* — *see page 54*

SOUTHERN INDIA

The temperature in Southern India is always high; the winters are never very cold and the summers are very hot indeed. The people are mainly vegetarian, and food tends to be much hotter than in the rest of India, probably because hot food helps to cool the body. The practice is to cook in oil rather than ghee, although some of the more elaborate Moghul dishes use ghee.

Most of Andhra Pradesh is on the high Deccan Plateau. In the past there was considerable Buddhist influence here. The Moghul rulers came down from the north as far south as Hyderabad and they too left their mark on Hyderabadi cooking.

One such example is Biriyani (Rice with lamb). This is among the most famous dishes of Hyderabad and is typical of rich Muslim cooking. It is made by marinating the lamb before cooking it and then layering it with parboiled rice and saffron. After this, live coals are placed on the lid of the pan until the rice is ready. In my recipe I have made it slightly easier, if slightly less authentic, by advocating cooking the dish in the oven (*see Hyderabadi biriyani for recipe*). Biriyani is normally eaten with Baghare baigan (Spiced eggplant) and Raita (Spiced yogurt). Here in Hyderabad the food tends to be very hot: green and red chilies are used profusely in the cooking. Another well-known and notoriously hot dish is Mirchi ka salan (Chili curry). You can make it less hot by first removing the seeds from the chilies, but be careful not to put your hands near your eyes afterwards, as chilies burn terribly. Rice, too, is grown here and is very popular.

Around Hyderabad, many monuments of Moghul architecture can still be seen, and many of them are encircled by crowded and lively bazaars.

Karnataka lies to the west of Andhra Pradesh. Here we find Bangalore, an industrial city, which contrasts sharply with the rural farming areas that surround it. The people are very friendly and take great pride in keeping their city clean and orderly. The majority of the incense manufactured in India is made in Mysore, some miles south west of Bangalore. Mysore is also famous for its crafts, particularly carvings of sandalwood, rosewood and teak. Ivory is also used in abundance. Rosewood coffee tables, noteworthy for their intricate work, are exported all over the world. This part of India is also famous for its silks, and the silk saris made in Bangalore are renowned all over India.

Kerala is a fertile coastal strip bordered by the Western Ghats, a low lying mountain range, which has protected Kerala from invaders. An agricultural state with very little heavy industry, there is a plentiful supply of rice and coconut growing here. Thanks to the abundance of coconut trees, coconut oil is used for cooking. Since this state is on the coast, seafood is popular and this, too, is prepared with coconut.

Kerala used to have a large Jewish population, and a large proportion of the spice trade takes place around the synagogue of Cochin. Kerala is one of the spice centers of India. The famous white sandy beach of Kovalam, surrounded by palm trees, is found here too. It is a spot of natural beauty, which the Indian government has developed into an interesting resort.

Tamil Nadu is the most southern state in India. The people are very hard working and friendly. In this part of the country you will see many Hindu temples, all built in the Dravidian style, which is characteristically ornate with soaring towers. In this state lies the hill station of Octacamund, or Ooty for short, which was used during the summer months by the British during the early nineteenth century. Before the British discovered it, however, the Todas, a tribal people, lived there, and a few Toda style huts can still be found there today. Ooty is in the Nilgiri mountain range, and in these mountains tea is grown.

Pondicherry is now famous for Sri Aurobindo's ashram. Until the middle of this century it was a French colony, but few traces of French culture remain.

Most people in the southern states drink a lot of fresh roasted coffee. Tea is not a favorite drink here, and, disliking small cups, the people of the south drink coffee from metal tumblers. They eat Dosas (Rice and lentil pancakes), Idlis (Steamed rice cakes) with Sambar (Lentils with vegetables) and Coconut chutney. The food tends to be very simple compared with that eaten in the north. Certain foods, such as Idli, are steamed, a practice virtually unheard of outside the southern states.

The non-vegetarians in the region eat meat dishes with coconut; for flavoring they add tamarind and curry leaves. A lot of rice, too, is eaten here. It is often served with Rasam (Lentils flavored with garlic) and Sambar (Lentils with vegetables). Rasam and sambar are made daily. Lentils are boiled in water until soft. The top part, which is mainly water, is strained off and used to cook the rasam and the thickened part is used for the sambar. Different seasonings are added to the rasam and sambar to finish cooking the dish.

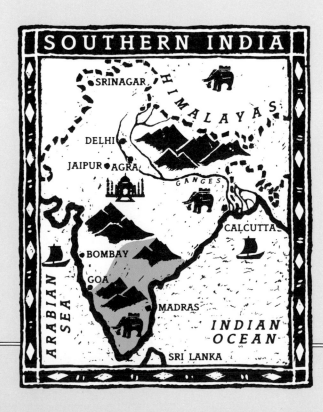

Rasam

Lentils flavored with garlic

PULSES

½ cup toovar dal
3¾ cups water
pinch of ground turmeric
1 tsp salt
2 tsp cumin seeds
1 tsp coriander seeds
½ tsp peppercorns
3–4 diced red chilies
1 cup tamarind juice
10–12 curry leaves
5 cloves garlic, crushed
1 tomato, chopped
1 tsp ghee
¼ tsp cumin seeds
4–6 curry leaves

1 Wash the toovar dal in several changes of water and bring to a boil in a large saucepan with the measured amount of water, turmeric and salt. Cover, leaving the lid slightly open, and simmer for about 30 minutes until the dal is soft. Blend until smooth.

2 In the meantime, dry roast the cumin, coriander, peppercorns and red chilies and grind finely.

3 Mix the tamarind juice, the powdered spices, curry leaves and garlic and bring to a boil. Simmer until it has reduced to half the amount.

4 Add the cooked dal and tomato and simmer for 5 minutes.

5 In a small saucepan, heat the ghee until very hot, add the ¼ tsp of cumin seeds and the curry leaves and let them sizzle for 5–6 seconds. Add to the cooked dal.

Serve very hot with rice or as a soup.

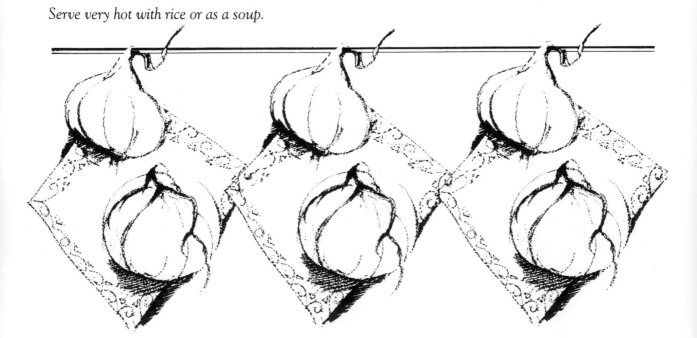

Idli

Steamed rice and lentil cake

⅓ cup urid dal, washed
1 cup rice, washed
good pinch of baking powder
pinch of salt

1 Soak the dal and rice separately in plenty of water for 4–5 hours. Drain.

2 In a liquidizer or food processor, grind the dal to a fine paste, adding a little water if necessary.

3 Grind the rice coarsely, adding a little water if necessary.

4 Mix the two pastes together well, cover and leave in a warm place overnight to let them ferment.

5 Mix in the baking powder and salt.

6 Fill the idli vessel* with the fermented mixture and steam for about 10 minutes until an inserted skewer comes out clean.

Serve with sambar.

* If you do not have a idli vessel, you can use egg poachers or custard cups.

Kootu

Lentils with vegetables

1 scant cup toovar dal, washed
3¾ cups water
½ tsp turmeric
1 tsp salt
½ cup carrots, scraped and diced
¼ cup peas (fresh or frozen)
½ cup French beans, cut into 1 in lengths
1 tbsp oil
1 tbsp urid dal
1 tsp peppercorns
2 dried red chilies, broken in half
10–12 curry leaves
4 tbsp coconut grated
¾ cup milk

1 Place the toovar dal, water, turmeric and salt in a saucepan and bring to a boil. Cover and simmer for about 35–40 minutes until the dal is soft. Add the vegetables and continue to cook until they are tender.

2 While the toovar dal is being cooked, heat the oil in a small saucepan and fry the urid dal, peppercorns, red chilies, curry leaves and coconut until the dal and coconut turn golden. Grind to a paste.

3 When the dal and vegetables are cooked, add the paste and milk and continue to cook for 5–10 minutes.

Serve hot with rice.

◆ *Lentils and beans (right) are displayed alongside creamy mounds of puffed and flaked rice in this pulse and grain merchant's store*

◆ **Kootu**/Lentils with vegetables *(below right)* — *see page 61*

◆ **Idli**/Steamed rice and lentil cakes *(below) are served with Sambar and Coconut chutney* — *see page 61*

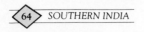

Sambar

LEGUMES

Lentils with vegetables

1 Place the toovar dal, water, 1 tsp of salt and turmeric in a large saucepan and bring to a boil. Lower the heat, cover, leaving the lid slightly ajar, and simmer for 35–40 minutes until the dal is soft.

2 In the meantime, heat ½ tbsp of oil in a small saucepan and fry the coriander seeds, channa dal and urid dal, 4 dried red chilies, fenugreek and asafetida, stirring constantly, until golden. (Take care that they do not get burnt.) Grind to a fine powder.

3 When the dal is soft, add the vegetables, tamarind juice and the remaining salt and continue to simmer until the vegetables are nearly tender.

4 Add the ground spices, stir well and cook for 5 minutes. Remove from the heat and put aside.

5 Heat the remaining 1 tbsp of oil in a small saucepan until very hot, add the mustard seeds and, when they stop spluttering, add the remaining dried red chilies broken in half and the curry leaves and let them fry for 4–5 seconds. Add this to the hot dal, give it a good stir and serve.

1 scant cup toovar dal, washed
4¼ cups water
2 tsp salt
½ tsp ground turmeric
1½ tbsp oil
4 tsp coriander seeds
1 tsp channa dal
1 tsp urid dal
6 dried red chilies
pinch of fenugreek seeds
good pinch of asafetida
1½ cups eggplant, cut into ½ in pieces
¾ cup French beans, cut into 1½ in lengths
6–8 shallots, peeled
½ cup tamarind juice
1 tsp mustard seeds
8–10 curry leaves

Baghare Baigan

VEGETABLES

Spiced eggplant

1 Place the onions directly on the open flame, or under a very hot broiler, with their skins still on, in order to roast them. Turn them often. As soon as the skins have turned black, remove from the fire and peel them, taking great care not to burn yourself.

2 Grind the onions with the coriander, 1 tsp cumin, sesame seeds, coconut and ¾ tsp fenugreek and put aside.

3 Wash the eggplant and dry.

4 Make two cuts in the eggplant crosswise from the top to

2 medium onions
¾ tsp coriander seeds
1½ tsp cumin seeds
1½ tsp sesame seeds
2 tbsp dry coconut
1¼ tsp fenugreek seeds
4 small long eggplant
¾ cup oil
½ tsp mustard seeds
6–8 curry leaves
½ in ginger, crushed
3 cloves garlic, crushed
½ tsp ground turmeric

about three-quarters of the way down towards the stalk, without cutting right through.

5 Heat the oil in a large skillet and fry the eggplant until browned and tender. Drain and put aside.

6 In the same oil add the remaining cumin, fenugreek, mustard and curry leaves and, as soon as the mustard starts to splutter, add the ginger, garlic, turmeric, chili and salt and stir fry for about 30 seconds.

7 Add the ground paste and continue to fry, stirring constantly, for 3–4 minutes until the oil floats to the top.

8 Add the tamarind juice, stir well and, after a minute, add the fried eggplant, and gently stir to coat the eggplant with the spices.

9 Cover and cook on a medium heat for about 10–15 minutes. Garnish with the coriander and mint.

Serve with Biriyani.

1 tsp chili powder
1 tsp salt
½ cup tamarind juice
1 tbsp coriander leaves, chopped
1 tbsp mint leaves, chopped

Avial

VEGETABLES

Vegetables in a yogurt and coconut sauce

1 In a large saucepan, place the bananas, vegetables, water, chili powder, turmeric and salt and bring to a boil. Simmer for about 20 minutes until the bananas and vegetables are tender. Remove from the heat.

2 Grind the green chilies, cumin seeds and coconut to a fine paste.

3 Add the paste to the yogurt and whisk until smooth.

4 In a large saucepan, heat the oil over a medium high heat, add the mustard seeds and curry leaves and, after 5–6 seconds, add the bananas and vegetables with the liquid and cook for 2–3 minutes. Lower the heat, add the yogurt mixture, and, stirring occasionally, cook for a further 4–5 minutes.

Serve with rice.

2 green bananas, peeled and cut into ½ in pieces
¼ lb/1 cup green beans, cut into 1 in lengths
½ cup carrots, diced into ¼ in cubes
¼ cup peas
1 cup okra, cut into 1 in lengths
1½ cups water
¾ tsp chili powder
½ tsp ground turmeric
¾ tsp salt
3 green chilies
1 tsp cumin seeds
½ a coconut
1 cup yogurt
1 tbsp oil
½ tsp mustard seeds
6–8 curry leaves

◆ **Avial**/Vegetables in a yogurt and coconut sauce *(above)* — *see page 65*

◆ **Baghare baigan**/Spiced eggplant *(above right) makes an excellent accompaniment to Hyderabadi Biriyani* — *see page 64*

◆ **Sambar**/Lentils with vegetables *(below right) is a staple dish of Southern India and is freshly made each morning* — *see page 64*

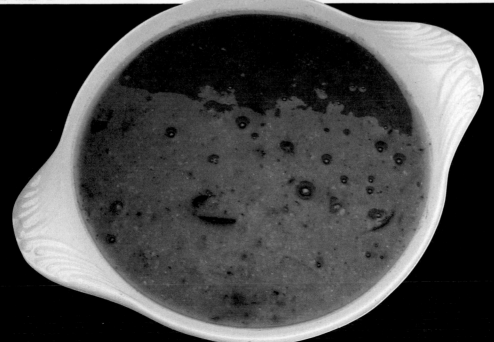

Mirchi Ka Salan

Chili curry

VEGETABLES

4 medium onions
1 lb green chilies
1/3 cup dried tamarind
1/2 tbsp molasses or brown sugar
1 cup hot water
4 tbsp dry coconut
2 tbsp sesame seeds
1 tbsp cumin seeds
1 1/2 tbsp coriander seeds
1 1/4 cups oil
1 tsp salt

1 Place the onions directly on the open flame with the skin still on, in order to roast them. (This can also be done under a very hot broiler.) Turn them often. As soon as the skins have turned black, remove from the heat and peel. Grind to a paste.

2 Slit the chilies lengthwise and remove the seeds.

3 Soak the tamarind and molasses in the hot water for 15–20 minutes. Squeeze the pulp and strain all the juice.

4 Dry roast the coconut, sesame, cumin and coriander until they are a few shades darker and a lovely aroma is given off. Grind to a fine powder.

5 Heat the oil in a saucepan over a medium high heat and fry the ground onions, stirring constantly, until lightly browned.

6 Add the powdered spices and stir fry for another 2–3 minutes.

7 Add the tamarind water, chilies and salt; when it starts to boil, lower the heat and cook until all the water has been absorbed and the oil floats on top.

If you want a really hot dish do not remove the seeds from the chilies.

Tamboda

Potatoes with tamarind juice

VEGETABLES

1 lb potatoes, boiled
1/2 cup tamarind juice
3/4 tsp chili powder
1 tsp salt
2 tsp oil
1/2 tsp mustard seeds
1/2 tsp fenugreek seeds
5–6 curry leaves

1 Cut the potatoes into 1/2 in cubes.

2 Place the potatoes, tamarind juice, chili powder and salt in a saucepan and bring to a boil over medium heat. Boil for 5–7 minutes. Remove from the heat.

3 Heat the oil in a small saucepan over a medium high heat. Add the mustard, fenugreek and curry leaves and let them sizzle for a few seconds. Add this mixture to the cooked potatoes, mix well and serve with rice.

Mandaraj Mulaku Nandoo

Madras pepper crab

FISH

10 tbsp oil
3 medium onions, finely sliced
1 large cooked crab, cut into pieces
1½ tbsp coarsely ground black pepper
1½ tsp salt

1 Heat the oil and fry the onions until soft and transparent.

2 Add the pieces of crab and fry with the onions for 3–4 minutes.

3 Add the pepper and salt and continue to fry for 8–10 minutes until cooked.

Serve with plain rice.

Mouli

Fish cooked in coconut milk

FISH

1½ lb white fish, cleaned
½ cup creamed coconut
1 cup boiling water
4 tbsp oil
3 cloves
1 medium onion, finely chopped
¼ tsp ground turmeric
1 tsp salt
3–4 green chilies
6–8 curry leaves

1 Cut the fish into 8–10 equal sized pieces.

2 Blend together the creamed coconut and water in a blender or food processor until smooth.

3 Heat the oil over a medium heat and fry the pieces of fish, a few at a time, until lightly browned. Keep on one side.

4 Add the cloves to the remaining oil. When they swell up, add the onion and fry until lightly golden. Add the turmeric and salt and stir fry for a few seconds.

5 Add the fish gently and mix.

6 Add the coconut milk and, when it starts to boil, cover, lower the heat to medium low and cook for about 10–12 minutes.

7 Add the chilies and curry leaves and cook for a further couple of minutes until the fish is tender.

Serve hot with rice. This dish can be also made with jumbo shrimp.

◆ **Erachi vella curry**/Meat stew *(above opposite)* *is a spicy lamb dish served hot with rice* *— see page 72*

◆ **Mirchi ka salan**/Chili curry *(below opposite),* *a fiery dish from Hyderabad — see page 68*

◆ *Freshly caught crab (left) is a great favorite in* *Southern India*

◆ **Mandaraj mulaku nandoo**/Madras pepper crab *(below) is simple to make and tastes delicious — see page 69*

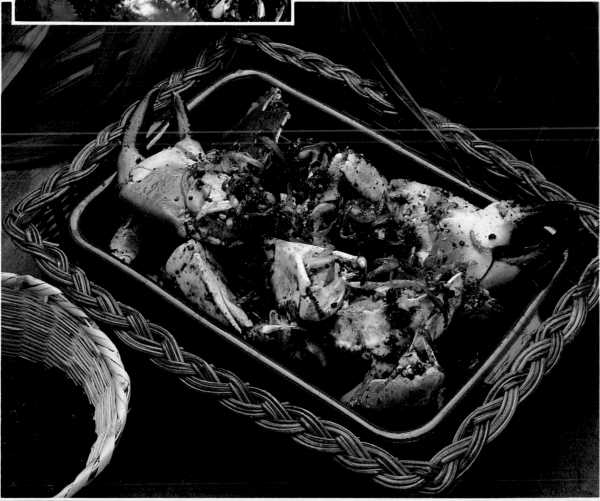

Erachi Vella Curry

Meat stew

1 Blend together the coconut and water until smooth.

2 In a large saucepan, put the lamb, chilies, ginger, onions, cinnamon, cloves, cardamom, curry leaves, salt and about 2 cups of the coconut milk and bring to a boil.

3 Cover, lower heat and simmer for 45 minutes. Add the remaining coconut milk and cook for a further 10 minutes. Remove from the heat.

4 In a small pan, heat the ghee and fry the onion until lightly browned. Add the pepper and the flour and, stirring constantly, mix the flour with the fried onion and ghee.

5 Add a little of the meat gravy and mix until smooth.

6 Add this to the stew and, stirring constantly, bring it to a boil.

Serve hot with rice.

⅔ cup creamed coconut
2½ cups hot water
2 lb/5⅓ cups lamb, cut into 1 in cubes
2–3 green chilies
1 in ginger, cut into thin strips
2 large onions, sliced
2 in piece of stick cinnamon
6 cloves
2 cardamom pods
6–7 curry leaves
1½ tsp salt
2 tbsp ghee
1 small onion, finely chopped
½ tsp freshly milled pepper
1 tbsp flour

Haleem

Meat cooked with wheat grains

1 Soak the wheat in plenty of water overnight. Drain. Place the wheat and some water in a large saucepan and bring to a boil. Cook until it is tender and mushy.

2 Grind the cardamom, cinnamon and cloves to a fine powder.

3 Grind the ginger and garlic to a fine paste.

4 In a large saucepan, heat the ghee and fry the onions until golden. Remove one third of the fried onions and put aside.

5 Add the ginger and garlic paste, the lamb, turmeric, chili powder, poppy seeds, dry coconut, coriander and mint leaves, the salt and half the ground spices and stir fry for 5–6 minutes.

1 lb/2 cups whole wheat grains
5 cardamom pods
1 in piece of stick cinnamon
6 cloves
1 in ginger
4 cloves garlic
¾ cup ghee
4 medium onions, finely sliced
1½ lb/4 cups boneless lamb, cut into 1 in cubes
1 tsp ground turmeric
2 tsp chili powder
1 tbsp ground poppy seeds
3 tbsp dry coconut, grated
2 tbsp coriander leaves, chopped
1 tbsp mint leaves, chopped

6 Add the yogurt and mix thoroughly. Lower the heat. Cover and cook for about 30 minutes.

7 Add the remaining ground spices and continue to cook for about another 30 minutes until the meat is tender. Remove from the heat.

8 Add the boiled wheat and beat with the back of a wooden spoon until the meat disintegrates.

9 Add the lime juice and stir well. Bring to a boil again and boil for 5 minutes.

10 Serve garnished with the remaining fried onions.

An alternative method is to lift the cooked meat out of the gravy and blend it with the wheat in a food processor, until coarsely ground. Then put it back into the gravy and continue from point 9 above.

2 tsp salt
¾ cup yogurt
juice of 2 limes

Hyderabadi Biriyani

MEAT

Rice with lamb

1 Wash the meat and leave in a colander to allow all the water to drain out.

2 Wash the rice in several changes of water. Soak for 15 minutes in water and then leave in a sieve to drain.

3 Blend the ginger, garlic, coriander, mint and green chilies to a fine paste.

4 Grind together 4 cloves, 1 piece of stick cinnamon, ½ tsp black cumin seeds, nutmeg and 3 cardamom pods to a fine powder.

5 Warm 2 tbsp milk and soak the saffron in it. Put aside.

6 Heat the ghee and fry the onions until golden brown. Drain and put aside.

7 Place the meat in a large bowl, add the coriander paste and, with the back of a wooden spoon, beat the meat for 15–20 minutes, turning the meat frequently.

2 lb/5⅓ cups lamb, cut into large pieces
2 lb/4 cups basmati rice
1 in ginger
4 cloves garlic
¼ cup coriander leaves
1 tbsp mint leaves
4 green chilies
8 cloves
2 × 1 in pieces of stick cinnamon
1 tsp black cumin seeds
¼ nutmeg
6 cardamom pods, skinned
6–8 tbsp milk
1 tsp saffron
⅔ cup ghee
3 large onions, halved and finely sliced
2 tsp chili powder
juice of 2 lemons
2 cups yogurt
3 tsp salt
12½ cups water
3 hard cooked eggs (optional) cut into quarters

8 To the meat add the chili powder, lemon juice, yogurt, 2 tsp salt, the powdered spices and half the fried onions, mix and put aside for 3–4 hours.

9 In a saucepan, melt the ghee again over a medium high heat and add the meat and the marinade. When it starts to boil, lower the heat, cover and, stirring occasionally, cook for about 1 hour until the meat is tender and the gravy thickened.

10 While the meat is being cooked, bring the water to a boil in a large saucepan. Add the remaining spices and 1 tsp salt.

11 When the water is boiling rapidly, add the drained rice, bring it back to a boil and boil the rice for 3–4 minutes until the rice is nearly cooked. Remove and drain the rice.

12 Lightly grease a large casserole dish big enough to hold all the rice and meat, and place half the cooked rice evenly at the bottom. Put the meat and gravy evenly on the rice and the remaining rice on top.

13 Sprinkle the saffron milk, the remaining milk and the rest of the fried onions on top. Cover tightly with aluminum foil and then the lid and place in a preheated oven at 375° F for about 45 minutes until the rice is cooked.

◆ **Hyderabadi biriyani**/Rice with lamb *is served with a Raita and Baghare baigan*

Masala Dosa

SNACK

Rice and lentil pancake with a potato stuffing

1 Soak the rice and urid dal separately in plenty of water and put aside for 6–8 hours. Drain.

2 In a liquidizer or food processor, blend the rice and dal separately to a fine paste. During the blending add a little water, if required.

3 Mix the two pastes together, add the salt and beat for 1–2 minutes.

4 Cover and keep aside in a warm place overnight to let it ferment.

5 Next morning, give the mixture a good stir and add enough

1 rounded cup rice, washed
1/3 cup urid dal, washed
1 tsp salt
about 3/4 cup water
a little oil for frying
Filling
4 tbsp oil
1/2 tsp mustard seeds
1 tbsp channa dal
1/3 tsp asafetida
2 tbsp cashew nuts, chopped (optional)
8–10 curry leaves
3/4 in ginger, grated
3–4 green chilies, chopped
1 large onion, finely sliced

water to make a thin pouring consistency.

Filling

1 Heat 4 tbsp oil in a saucepan over a medium high heat, add the mustard seeds, channa dal, asafetida, cashew nuts, curry leaves, ginger and green chilies and let them sizzle for 6–8 seconds.

2 Add the onion and fry until transparent.

3 Add the potatoes, turmeric and salt and mix with the other spices. Add the water, bring to a boil, cover and simmer over a medium heat for about 10 minutes until well mixed and all the water has evaporated. Put aside.

Making the pancakes

1 Heat a non stick skillet over a medium heat and brush with a little oil. Pour in a ladleful of the mixture and spread it like a pancake. Put a little more oil around the edges and a little on top. Cook for a couple of minutes until lightly golden. Turn the dosa and cook for a further couple of minutes.

2 Put on a plate, place a heaped tablespoon of the hot filling on one end of the dosa, fold in half and serve hot with coconut chutney and sambar. (It can also be folded to make a triangle.)

1 lb/4 cups potatoes, peeled and diced into ¼ in cubes and then boiled
½ tsp ground turmeric
1 tsp salt
½ cup water

◆ **Masala dosa**/Rice and lentil pancake with a potato stuffing *is served hot with Coconut chutney and Sambar*

Uppuma

SNACK

Savory semolina

1 Dry roast the semolina until lightly golden. Put aside.

2 Dry roast the peanuts until golden and put aside.

3 Heat the oil over a medium heat, add the mustard seeds, urid and channa dals and when they stop spluttering, add the onion and 8 of the curry leaves, and fry until the onion is golden in color.

4 Add the vegetables and stir fry for 2–3 minutes.

5 Add the semolina and mix with the other ingredients and continue to fry for a further 1–2 minutes.

1 cup coarse semolina
2 tbsp unsalted peanuts, chopped
3 tbsp oil
¼ tsp mustard seeds
1 tsp urid dal
1 tsp channa dal
1 medium onion, finely chopped
10–12 curry leaves
1 small carrot, cut into thin strips about 2 in long
2 tbsp peas
4–5 French beans, cut into thin strips about 2 in long
1 tsp salt
about 3 cups water
juice of ½ a lemon

6 Add the salt and water and, stirring constantly, cook until all the water evaporates and the mixture is absolutely dry.

7 Squeeze on the lemon juice and mix in the remaining curry leaves.

8 Garnish with the roasted peanuts.

Serve hot with Coconut chutney as a light meal.

Vada

Fried lentil cakes

1 Soak the dal in plenty of cold water for 4–5 hours. Drain.

2 Grind the dal coarsely in a food processor or blender. (If using a blender, add a little water only if necessary.)

3 To the ground dal, add the green chilies, onions, asafetida, chili powder and salt and mix well.

4 Heat oil over a medium high heat.

5 Take a tablespoon of the mixture in the palm of your hand and flatten it slightly and deep fry for 1–2 minutes until golden brown.

Serve hot.

1 scant cup channa dal, washed
1–2 green chilies, chopped
1 small onion, finely chopped
pinch of asafetida
½ tsp chili powder (optional)
½ tsp salt
oil for deep frying

Pulisharam

Tamarind rice

1 Wash the rice in several changes of water and soak for 20 minutes. Drain.

2 Place the rice and measured amount of water in a saucepan and bring to a boil over a high heat. Lower the heat to very low, cover and cook for about 20 minutes until all the water has evaporated and the rice is cooked. Remove from the heat and fluff with a fork.

3 Heat 1 tbsp of the oil in a large skillet and fry the channa dal

1 cup basmati rice
2 cups water
2 tbsp oil
1 tbsp channa dal
2 tsp mustard seeds
¼ tsp fenugreek seeds
2 tbsp unsalted peanuts
pinch of asafetida
½ tsp ground turmeric
½ cup tamarind juice
1½ tsp salt

and 1 tsp of the mustard seeds until the dal turns golden. Add the cooked rice, mix well and remove from the fire.

4 Dry roast the fenugreek seeds and grind to a fine powder. Dry roast the peanuts and put aside.

5 In a large saucepan, heat the remaining oil, add the mustard seeds, peanuts, asafetida and turmeric and fry for a few seconds, taking care that the spices do not burn.

6 Add the tamarind juice and salt and cook until the mixture becomes thick. Add the powdered fenugreek, and stir to mix.

7 Add the rice and mix gently, cover and cook on a very low heat for 5 minutes.

Serve hot or cold.

Thasikaysharan

Lime rice

RICE

1 cup rice
1 tbsp channa dal
1 tbsp urid dal
2 cups water
¼ tsp ground turmeric
½ tsp fenugreek seeds
½ tsp asafetida
2 tbsp oil
1 tbsp unsalted cashew nuts
¾ tsp mustard seeds
2 green chilies, chopped
6–8 curry leaves
1 tsp salt
juice of 1 lime

1 Wash the rice in several changes of water and soak in plenty of water for 30 minutes. Drain.

2 Wash the channa and urid dals and soak in plenty of water for 30 minutes. Drain.

3 Place the rice and the measured amount of water in a saucepan with the turmeric and bring to a boil. Lower the heat to very low, cover and cook for about 20 minutes until the rice is cooked and all the water evaporated.

4 Dry roast the fenugreek and asafetida and grind to a fine powder.

5 Heat the oil in a large skillet, add the cashew nuts, mustard, chilies, curry leaves and the drained dals; fry until the dals are golden in color.

6 Add the cooked rice, salt and lime juice and, stirring gently, mix well. Sprinkle with the ground spices.

Serve hot or cold.

◆ **Vada**/Fried lentil cakes *(left)*
— *see page 76*

TYPICAL MENUS

Masala dosa

Sambar

Thankai chutney

Payasam

★ ★ ★

Hyderabadi biriyani

Baghare baigan

Raita

◆ **Uppuma**/Savory semolina — *see page 75*

Thankai Chutney

Coconut chutney

1 Soak the tamarind in the hot water for 30 minutes. Squeeze well to draw out all the pulp. Strain.

2 In a liquidizer or food processor, blend together the coconut, tamarind juice, green chilies and ginger until fairly fine.

3 In a small saucepan, heat the oil. Add the mustard seeds, red chilies and curry leaves and let them sizzle for 5–6 seconds. Add this to the blended mixture and stir well to mix.

Green food coloring can also be added for variety.

1½ tbsp dried tamarind
¼ cup hot water
½ coconut, grated
1–2 green chilies
½ in ginger
2 tsp oil
½ tsp mustard seeds
2 dried red chilies
4–5 curry leaves

Payasam

South Indian creamed rice

1 Wash the rice and set aside in a sieve to drain for 20 minutes.

2 Bring the milk to a boil, in a large saucepan, stirring constantly.

3 Lower the heat, add the rice and stir well to mix.

4 Simmer until the rice is tender and the milk slightly thickened.

5 Add the jaggery or brown sugar, stir to mix and simmer for a further 5-7 minutes.

6 Stir in the cashew nuts and remove from the heat.

½ cup rice
5 cups milk
½ cup jaggery (raw palm sugar) or brown sugar
1 tbsp cashew nuts, roasted

CENTRAL INDIA

Central India includes the states of Rajasthan, Madhya Pradesh, Uttar Pradesh and Bihar. The women of the region are very colourfully dressed — they wear bright skirts featuring beautiful mirrorwork, and lots of chunky jewellery. And the men top their outfits with huge, pastel-coloured turbans and sport fantastic moustaches.

Rajasthan is situated in the north west of India. Literally, the name means 'land of the kings' and it is the home not of kings but of the warrior clans called Rajputs. The Rajputs were once noted for their bravery and sense of honor but were always too disorganized ever to pose a serious threat to the successive oppressors or conquerors of India. Their women were equally brave—perhaps even more so. One example of their bravery is shown by the ritual, "Jauhar", if a warrior husband was killed in battle, his wife would build a funeral pyre and commit suicide.

In Rajasthan is the Thar Desert, which extends across the border to Pakistan. This area is dry and inhospitable but the south east region is hilly and quite picturesque.

Jaipur is the capital of the region and many ruined forts and palaces remain in this princely state. Two large palaces have been converted into luxury hotels, and the one in Udaipur, known as the Lake Palace Hotel, is built in the middle of a lake and is magnificent. The other, the Rambagh Palace Hotel, is also beautiful and is to be found in Jaipur, the pink city. Jaipur is known as the pink city because the buildings were built with pink-colored sandstone.

Besides the Rajputs, another community can be found here: the Marwaris. They are followers of Jainism and therefore strict vegetarians; they use lots of ghee in their cooking and eat gram flour and legumes.

A meal for the Marwaris involves a little rice and a few pooris with dal, two different kinds of vegetables, one dry and the other with gravy, small amounts of three or four different pickles, pappadoms and sweetmeats. Marwaris are known for the wonderful pappadoms they make: a few women gather together skillfully and pleasurably to make enough pappadoms in one sitting to last an entire year. It may sound like hard work but they enjoy it and gently sing together while they roll out the dough. In Europe, however, people tend to buy pappadoms ready-made.

During the dry, hot summers, when hardly any vegetables are available, the Marwaris eat different kinds of breads with pickles *(see Breads and Rice, and Accompaniments, for recipes)*, or they make a dough with gram flour, roll it, boil it, and then make a curry of it or cook it with rice; this is called Gatte ki saag or Gatte ki khichiri. The dishes are simple, but extremely tasty.

Madhya Pradesh is right in the center of India, and most of the state lies on a high plateau. The summers are very hot and dry. People came from other places around the state to settle here, and there are therefore strong influences of Gujarathi, Marathi and Uttar Pradesh in the regional cuisine. However, most of the people are Hindus and so the predominant tongue is Hindi.

Uttar Pradesh has elements of both Hindu and Muslim cultures. It is a highly populated state. To the north east are the Himalayas and it is from here that the sacred Hindu river, the Ganges, begins. The holy city of the Hindus, Varanasi, sits on the banks of the Ganges. Pilgrims come from all over India to take a dip in the holy water and cleanse away their sins. Mathura is another important place for pilgrimages and is believed to be the site where Lord Krishna was born, about 3,000 years ago.

Muslim influence is particularly strong in Lucknow, a city famous for its Moghlai cuisine. Mouth watering kebobs are a speciality: some are made with ground meat under the broiler (Seekh kabab); others comprise ground meat boiled with lentils, drained, blended with spices and then fried in oil (Shami kabab); still others involve cubes of lamb, marinated and then broiled (Boti kabab). All these kebobs are usually eaten with breads. The area is also known for its delightful biriyanis and meat dishes. A favorite dessert is Zaffrani chawal (Saffron rice), which is sweetened rice flavored with saffron and nuts.

The Moghuls constructed some splendid buildings, many of which are, unfortunately, in ruins. However, the best one still exists today: the Taj Mahal in Agra, built by Shah Jahan for his beloved wife Mumtaz Mahal upon her death, was built in marble and inlaid with semi precious stones. It stands right beside the Yamuna River and its glorious reflection can be seen in the waters, subtly changing color as the sun rises and sets.

The plains of Uttar Pradesh are fertile and well irrigated by the Ganges although sometimes, during the monsoons, they flood. The people live and eat simply. They enjoy many different kinds of legumes and cook them imaginatively. For example, they boil lentils with turmeric and salt and when the lentils are soft, they add a tarka (a mixture of spices and hot oil or ghee), in this case comprising asafetida, cumin seeds, dried red chilies and chili powder. They also cook lentils with spinach or fenugreek leaves, and Raita (Spiced yogurt — *see Accompaniments for recipe*) is eaten in plenty with nearly all meals. For breakfast they have Kachoris (Stuffed pooris — *see Breads and Rice for recipe*) and chutneys (*see Accompaniments for recipe*).

Generally, wedding feasts in villages in the Uttar Pradesh have the following menu: Rasadar aloo (Spicy potatoes), Kaddu ki sabzi (Pumpkin with spices), Sukha aloo (Dry potatoes), Matar pillau (Pea pilaf), Poori (Deep fried brown bread), Boondi raita (Yogurt with fried gram flour batter), Sonth (Tamarind chutney) and, finally Jelebis (Fried sweets in syrup).

On the eastern side of Uttar Pradesh is the state of Bihar. The capital, now known as Patna, was once called Pataliputra, the ancient seat of learning. Centuries ago the area flourished but today it is overpopulated and poor. The people eke out their livelihood from growing rice, and their staple food is the local grain, sattu. It is kneaded with a little oil and eaten with green chilies and pickle.

Their meat and vegetable cookery has been influenced by Uttar Pradesh and their fish dishes show elements of Bengali cooking. Both in Uttar Pradesh and Bihar, mustard oil is the preferred cooking medium.

CENTRAL INDIA

Arhar Dal (Toovar Dal)

Spicy lentils

1 scant cup toovar dal
3¾ cups water
½ tsp ground turmeric
1 tsp salt
1 tsp ghee
1 tsp cumin seeds
2 dried red chilies, broken into 2
a pinch of asafetida
½ tsp chili powder
2 tbsp coriander leaves, chopped

1 Wash the toovar dal in several changes of water and drain. Bring to a boil in the measured amount of water, with the turmeric and salt, over a high heat.

2 Lower the heat, cover, leaving the lid slightly open, and simmer for about 40 minutes until tender.

3 In a small pan, heat the ghee. Add the cumin seeds, and dried red chilies and let them sizzle for 10 seconds; add the asafetida and chili powder and let them sizzle for 3–4 seconds. Add this to the hot dal and mix well.

4 Garnish with the coriander leaves.

Kachori

Stuffed, spiced pastries

Filling
½ cup urid dal, washed
1 tsp ghee
1 tsp salt
¼ tsp fennel seeds
½ in piece of stick cinnamon
½ black cardamom pod, skinned
6 peppercorns
pinch of asafetida
pinch of ground ginger
¼ tsp ground cumin
½ tsp chili powder
Dough
2 cups wholewheat flour
1 tsp salt
2 tsp melted ghee
½ cup hot water
oil for deep frying

Filling

1 Soak the dal in plenty of cold water overnight.

2 Drain and blend to a smooth paste, adding a little water if necessary.

3 Heat the ghee in a karai, add the dal paste and salt and, stirring constantly, fry until the mixture leaves the side and forms a lump. Keep on one side.

4 Grind together the fennel, cinnamon, black cardamom and peppercorns to a fine powder.

5 Add this and all the remaining spices to the dal and mix.

Dough

1 Mix the wholewheat flour and salt.

2 Rub the ghee into the flour/salt mixture.

3 Add enough hot water to make a soft, pliable dough. Knead for about 10 minutes.

4 Divide the dough into 12–14 balls.

5 Take one ball, flatten slightly and make a depression in the middle with your thumb, to form a cup shape. Fill the center with the spiced dal mixture and re-form the pastry ball, making sure that the edges are well gathered. Flatten the ball slightly between the palms of your hands.

6 Heat the oil in a karai over a medium heat and fry the kachoris a few at a time for 7–8 minutes until they are lightly browned.

Serve with pickle.

Dahi Vada

Lentil cakes in yogurt

1 Wash the dal and soak in the water overnight.

2 Put the dal, green chilies, salt and asafetida and enough of the soaking liquid into a liquidizer or food processor and blend until you have a thick paste.

3 In a karai or saucepan, heat the oil over a medium high heat.

4 Put tablespoonfuls of the mixture into the hot oil and fry for 3–4 minutes until they are reddish brown, turning once. Drain them on paper towels.

5 When all the vadas have been fried, put them in a bowl of warm water for 1 minute. Squeeze out the water gently and put in a large dish.

6 Combine the yogurt, roasted cumin, garam masala and chili powder and mix until smooth. Pour over the vadas.

Chill and serve with Tamarind chutney.

LEGUMES

1 cup urid dal, washed
about 2 cups water
3 green chilies
½ tsp salt
¼ tsp asafetida
oil for deep frying
3¾ cups yogurt
1 tsp ground roasted cumin
¼ tsp garam masala
½ tsp chili powder

◆ **Dahi vada**/Lentil cakes in yogurt *(left)*
are served chilled with Tamarind chutney
— see page 85

◆ **Kaddu ki sabzi**/Pumpkin with spices *(below)*
is a tasty vegetable accompaniment —
see page 87

Kaddu Ki Sabzi

VEGETABLES

Pumpkin with spices

1 Peel the pumpkin and cut into 1 in cubes. Wash and drain.

2 Heat the oil in a saucepan over a medium high heat. Add the fenugreek and, as soon as it starts to splutter, add the pumpkin, turmeric, chili and salt. Stir fry for 1 minute.

3 Lower the heat, cover and cook for about 15–20 minutes, stirring occasionally, until the pumpkin is soft and pulpy.

4 Add the sugar and mango powder, mix into the pumpkin and cook a further 1–2 minutes.

5 Sprinkle on the garam masala and serve hot.

1½ lb pumpkin
3 tbsp oil
1 tsp fenugreek seeds
½ tsp ground turmeric
1 tsp chili powder
1 tsp salt
2 tsp sugar
1½ tsp mango powder
½ tsp garam masala

Mooli Ki Sabzi

VEGETABLES

Spicy white radish with yogurt

1 Chop the radish, including the tender leaves, into small cubes.

2 Boil the radish in water for 20 minutes. Drain.

3 Heat the ghee in a saucepan over a medium heat, add the mustard, cumin and asafetida and let them sizzle for 5–6 seconds.

4 Remove from the heat, and add the yogurt and the remaining spices.

5 Stirring constantly, return to the heat, making sure that the yogurt does not separate. Cook for 1 minute.

6 Add the water; when it comes to a boil, add the radish and mix in with the spices.

7 Cook for about 8–10 minutes.

1½ lb white radish, washed and scraped
3 tbsp ghee
½ tsp mustard seeds
¼ tsp cumin seeds
pinch of asafetida
½ cup yogurt, lightly beaten
3 tsp ground coriander
½ tsp ground turmeric
1 tsp chili powder
1 tsp mango powder
about ⅓ cup water

Sabu Bhindi

VEGETABLES

Fried, stuffed okra

1 Wash the okra and dry thoroughly, otherwise it will not fry fry very well.

2 Mix together the cumin, turmeric, chili, mango powder and salt.

3 Make a pocket in each okra by cutting a slit of about 2 in lengthwise along one side, making sure you do not cut right through. By pushing the ends gently you will make a small pocket.

4 Put a little bit of the spice mixture into the pocket.

5 When all the okra has been filled, heat the oil in a large skillet over a medium high heat and add the okra.

6 Fry for 5 minutes, stirring gently.

7 Lower the heat, cover and cook for a further 10 minutes until the okra is golden all over.

If there is any spice remaining after the okra has been filled, sprinkle it on top of the okra while it is cooking.

1 lb large okra
1 tbsp ground cumin
½ tsp ground turmeric
½ tsp chili powder
1 tbsp mango powder
1 tsp salt
4–5 tbsp oil

Rasadar Aloo

VEGETABLES

Spicy potatoes

1 Peel the potatoes and wash them.

2 Place the tomatoes in boiling water for 10 seconds. Carefully peel and chop them.

3 Heat the oil over a medium high heat in a karai or saucepan. Add the cumin seeds and asafetida and let them sizzle for 5–6 seconds.

4 Add the chopped tomatoes, turmeric, coriander, chili, paprika and salt and, stirring constantly, fry for 30 seconds. (If it starts to stick to the bottom, sprinkle on a little water.)

1½ lb small potatoes
2–3 medium tomatoes
4 tbsp oil
1 tsp cumin seeds
pinch of asafetida
¾ tsp ground turmeric
1 tsp ground coriander
¾ tsp chili powder
1 tsp paprika
1 tsp salt
1¼ cups water
½ tsp garam masala
2 tbsp coriander leaves, chopped

5 Add the potatoes and fry for 2–3 minutes, stirring constantly.

6 Add the water and bring to a boil. Lower the heat, cover and cook for about 15 minutes until the potatoes are tender.

7 Add the garam masala and mix.

8 Remove and garnish with the coriander leaves.

Sukha Aloo

VEGETABLES

Dry potatoes

1 Boil the potatoes with the skins still on. Peel and cut into large pieces (make sure you do not overcook them).

2 Heat the oil in a karai or saucepan over a medium high heat. Add the cumin seeds and asafetida and let them sizzle for about 5–6 seconds.

3 Add the turmeric, chili, coriander, mango powder and salt and fry for 5–7 seconds. If it starts to stick, sprinkle a little water on the mixture.

4 Add the potatoes and, stirring gently, fry for 5 minutes.

1½ lb potatoes, washed
4 tbsp oil
1 tsp cumin seeds
pinch of asafetida
¾ tsp ground turmeric
¾ tsp chili powder
1 tsp ground coriander
1 tsp mango powder
1 tsp salt

Murgh Biriyani

CHICKEN

Spicy chicken with rice

1 Skin the chicken and cut into 8–10 pieces. Wash and pat dry.

2 Wash the rice several times, changing the water each time, and soak in plenty of water for 20 minutes. Drain and keep aside.

3 Finely slice three of the onions and chop the remaining one.

4 In a blender or food processor, blend the coriander leaves, almonds, garlic, ginger and green chilies to a smooth paste.

5 Heat 5 tbsp of ghee in a large saucepan over a medium high

2½ lb chicken
1½ lb rice
4 medium onions
1½ tbsp coriander leaves, washed
3 tbsp almonds
3 cloves garlic
½ in ginger
4 green chilies
6 tbsp ghee
3 tbsp cashew nuts
8–10 small potatoes, peeled and washed
1½ tsp ground cumin
1½ tsp ground coriander

◆ **Rasadar aloo/**
Spicy potatoes *(right)*
— see page 88

◆ *A market trader awaits custom
for his potatoes, onions and garlic
(opposite)*

◆ **Sukha aloo/**Dry potatoes
(right) — see page 89

heat and add the cashew nuts. Fry the nuts until golden; remove and keep on one side.

6 Fry the potatoes until they are lightly browned all over. Remove from the heat and keep on one side.

7 Fry the sliced onions till golden brown. Drain.

8 Add the chopped onion to the remaining oil and fry until lightly golden.

9 Add the fresh coriander paste, cumin, ground coriander, chili powder, garam masala and 1 tsp salt and stir fry for one minute.

10 Add the pieces of chicken and mix with the spices. Stir fry for 2–3 minutes. Reduce the heat to medium and continue to cook for a further 5 minutes.

11 Add the cup of water. When it starts to boil, lower the heat, cover and cook for 15 minutes.

12 Add the fried potatoes and cook for a further 15–20 minutes, until the potatoes are tender and the gravy thickened.

13 While the chicken is being cooked, warm the milk and soak the saffron in it.

14 Bring the 4 pts of water to the boil in a large saucepan. Add the remaining salt. When the water is boiling rapidly, add the drained rice and bring it back to the boil. Boil for 3–4 minutes until the rice is nearly done. Remove from the heat and drain.

15 With the remaining ghee, grease a large casserole dish and place half the rice evenly in the bottom. Next add the chicken and gravy and finally the remaining rice.

16 Sprinkle the saffron milk on top of the rice. Place the fried onions and cashew nuts on top, cover tightly with aluminum foil and then the lid and place in a pre-heated oven 375°F for about 45 minutes until the rice is cooked.

Serve hot garnished with the eggs.

1½ tsp chili powder
½ tsp ground garam masala
2 tsp salt
1 cup water
6 tbsp milk
½ tsp saffron thread
4 pts water
3 hard cooked eggs (optional), cut into quarters lengthwise

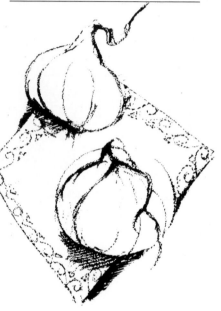

Seekh Kabab

MEAT

Lamb kebob

1 Cut the lamb into 1 in cubes.

2 In a blender or food processor, blend together the onion, garlic and ginger, adding a little water if necessary.

3 Grind the cinnamon, cardamom, poppy seeds, nutmeg, clove and peppercorns to a fine powder.

4 Place the lamb in a large bowl, add the onion paste, powdered spices, salt, chili powder and yogurt, and mix thoroughly. Cover the bowl with plastic wrap and place in the refrigerator overnight to marinate.

5 Divide the meat between 6 skewers.

6 Place under a hot broiler and baste occasionally with the ghee. Turn once or twice and cook until tender—about 10 minutes.

Serve hot with Onion salad and wedges of lemon.

1 lb/2⅔ cups lean, boneless lamb
1 medium onion
3 cloves garlic
1 in ginger
1 in piece of stick cinnamon
2 cardamom pods, skinned
1 tsp poppy seeds
⅛ nutmeg
1 clove
2 peppercorns
1 tsp salt
1 tsp chili powder
¼ pt/125 ml yogurt
ghee for basting

Gosht Curry

MEAT

Simple lamb curry

1 Wash and dry the meat. Cut into 1 in cubes.

2 In a blender or food processor, blend together the onion, garlic and ginger to a fine paste.

3 Place the tomatoes in boiling water for 10 seconds. Peel and chop the tomatoes, and put aside.

4 Heat the ghee in a large saucepan and fry the onion paste, stirring constantly, until golden brown.

5 Add the coriander, cumin, chili, garam masala and salt and stir fry for 1–2 minutes.

6 Add the meat and fry for a few minutes with the spices.

1 lb/2⅔ cups boneless lamb
3 onions
4 cloves garlic
1 in ginger
3 tomatoes
3 tbsp ghee
2 tsp ground coriander
1½ tsp ground cumin
1 tsp chili powder
½ tsp garam masala
1 tsp salt
¼ cup yogurt, lightly beaten
1 cup water

◆ **Gosht curry**/Simple lamb curry *(above)* is a *spicy main course dish — see page 93*

◆ **Seekh kabab**/Lamb kebob *(left) set against the stately setting of the Rambagh Palace, Jaipur — see page 93*

7 Add the yogurt, mix well and fry for a further minute.

8 Add the water and, when it starts to boil, lower the heat; cover and cook for about 40 minutes, stirring occasionally.

9 Add the tomatoes, stir well to mix, cover again and cook for a further 25–30 minutes until the meat is tender and the gravy slightly thickened.

Shami Kabab

MEAT

Lamb and lentil kebob

1 In a saucepan, place the ground lamb, channa dal, cardamom, peppercorns, onions, garlic, ginger, chili powder, salt and water; bring to a boil over a medium high heat.

2 Cover, lower the heat and simmer until the dal is tender and all the water absorbed.

3 Place the mixture in a food processor or liquidizer and blend until smooth.

4 Mix in the beaten egg, and divide into 16–18 small balls.

5 Combine the ingredients for the filling and put aside.

6 Take a ground lamb and dal ball, and with your thumb, make a depression in the middle to form a cup shape. Fill the center with a little filling and re-form into a smooth ball. Flatten slightly.

7 Heat the oil in a large skillet and fry the kebobs, turning once until nicely browned. Drain.

Serve hot with Onion salad and wedges of lemon.

1 lb/2 cups lean, ground lamb
⅓ cup channa dal, washed and drained
2 large black cardamom pods, skinned
6 black peppercorns
1 medium onion, chopped
3 cloves garlic, crushed
1 in ginger, grated
½ tsp chili powder
1 tsp salt
about ½ cup water
1 egg, lightly beaten
Stuffing
1 medium onion, finely chopped
3 green chilies, chopped
3 tbsp coriander leaves, chopped
oil for frying

Gatte Ki Saag

SNACK

Curry with gram flour dumplings

Dough

1 Place the gram flour, chili powder, coriander, turmeric and salt in a bowl. Rub in the ghee.

Dough
¾ cup gram flour
¼ tsp chili powder
½ tsp ground coriander

2 Add enough water to make a firm dough. Knead for 2–3 minutes.

3 Divide into 4 parts. Roll each ball between your palms into 6 in long, round strips.

4 Bring some water to a boil, and place these strips into the water carefully. Boil for 5 minutes. Drain and cool. Cut into ½ in pieces.

Curry

1 Heat the ghee in a saucepan over a medium heat. Add the cumin seeds, mustard and asafetida and let them splutter for 5–6 seconds.

2 Remove from the heat and add yogurt and the rest of the spices.

3 Stirring constantly, return the pan to the heat and cook for about 3–4 minutes (if you do not stir constantly the yogurt might separate).

4 Add the gram flour pieces, mix gently with the gravy and cook for a further 5 minutes.

good pinch of turmeric

¾ tsp salt

2 tbsp melted ghee

about ¼ cup water

Curry

2 tbsp melted ghee

½ tsp cumin seeds

¼ tsp mustard seeds

pinch of asafetida

½ cup yogurt, beaten well

½ tsp chili powder

3 tsp ground coriander

½ tsp ground turmeric

1 tsp salt

Gatte Ki Khichiri

SNACK

Rice with gram flour dumplings

1 Sieve the gram flour into a large bowl.

2 Mix in the chili powder, coriander, turmeric and half the salt. Rub in the ghee.

3 Add enough water to make a firm dough, knead for 2–3 minutes.

4 Divide into 4 parts. Roll each ball between your palms into 6 in long, round strips.

5 Bring some water to a boil and place these strips carefully in the water. Boil for 5 minutes. Drain and cool—cut into ½ in pieces.

¾ cup gram flour

¼ tsp chili powder

½ tsp ground coriander

pinch of turmeric

½ tsp salt

2 tbsp hot, melted ghee

about ¼ cup hot water

Rice

1½ cups basmati rice

2 tbsp ghee

1 tsp cumin seeds

½ tsp chili powder

3¾ cups boiling water

Rice

1 Wash the basmati rice in several changes of water. Soak for 20 minutes in plenty of water and then drain.

2 In a large saucepan, heat the ghee over a medium high heat. Add the cumin seeds and let them sizzle for 3–4 seconds.

3 Add the rice, chili powder and remaining salt, and sauté for 2–3 minutes.

4 Add the gram flour pieces carefully and gently mix with the rice. Fry for 1 minute.

5 Add the water and, when it starts to boil rapidly, lower the heat to very low, cover and cook for about 20 minutes until the rice is tender.

6 Fluff with a fork and serve hot.

◆ **Gatte ki khichiri**/Rice with gram flour dumplings — *see page 97*

◆ **Shami kabab**/Lamb and lentil kebob, *served with Onion salad — see page 96*

Phalon Ki Chaat

Fruit salad

1 Cut the fruit and vegetables into bite size pieces.

2 Place in a bowl, sprinkle with Chaat masala and lime juice and mix gently.

Serve immediately at the beginning of a meal or as a refreshing snack.

2 bananas
1 large tomato
1 apple
1 orange
1 large potato, boiled
⅓ cucumber
2–3 tsp Chaat masala
1 tbsp lime juice

Kairi Ki Laungi

Green mangoes in spicy syrup

1 Wash the mangoes and cut them lengthwise into quarters (do not peel). Remove the seeds.

2 Heat the oil over a medium high heat, add the cumin, mustard, asafetida, fennel, coriander and fenugreek and let them sizzle for a few seconds.

3 Add the mangoes, turmeric and chili; stir to mix all the spices and cook for 2 minutes.

4 Add the water and sugar, bring to a boil, lower the heat and simmer for about 5 minutes.

3 small green mangoes
2 tbsp oil
½ tsp cumin seeds
½ tsp mustard seeds
pinch of asafetida
¼ tsp fennel seeds
¼ tsp coriander seeds
¼ tsp fenugreek seeds
pinch of ground turmeric
½ tsp chili powder
1 cup water
3 tbsp sugar

Serve hot.

Besan Laddu

Gram flour balls

1 Sieve the gram flour.

2 Heat the ghee in a heavy based saucepan over a medium heat and fry the gram flour until golden.

3 Remove from the heat and cool. Add sugar and mix well.

4 When cold, make into small balls about the size of a walnut.

1 cup gram flour
6 tbsp ghee
½ cup sugar

Zaffrani Chawal

Saffron rice

1 Wash the rice in several changes of water and soak in water for 15 minutes. Place the rice in a sieve to drain thoroughly.

2 Soak the saffron in 2 tbsp of the boiling water for 15 minutes.

3 Heat the ghee in a large saucepan over a medium high heat; add the cardamom and let it sizzle for 3–4 seconds. Add the drained rice and almonds and, stirring constantly, fry for 3–4 minutes until lightly golden.

4 Add the boiling water, saffron and sugar and stir to mix. Lower the heat to very low, cover and cook for about 20 minutes until all the water has been absorbed and the rice is tender.

5 Fluff with a fork, garnish with pistachio nuts and serve.

1½ cups basmati rice
½ tsp saffron
about 4 cups boiling water
5 tbsp ghee
2–3 cardamom pods
4 tbsp almonds, slivered
5 tbsp sugar
1 tbsp pistachio nuts, chopped

Jelebi

Fried sweets in syrup

1 Sieve together the flour and baking powder. Add the yogurt and mix well. Add enough milk to make a thick batter of pouring consistency. Keep aside in a warm place overnight.

2 When you are ready to fry the jelebis, prepare the syrup. Place the sugar and water in a large saucepan and bring to a boil. Boil for 5–6 minutes until it becomes slightly thick. Remove from the heat and add coloring and rose water. Stir well and keep aside.

3 Heat the oil over a medium high heat.

4 Place the batter into a piping bag with a ¼ in plain nozzle. Squeeze the batter into the hot oil, making spiral shapes of about 2½ in in diameter.

5 Fry until golden. Drain and add to the syrup for 1 minute. Remove from the syrup.

1¼ cups plain flour
½ tsp baking powder
2 tbsp water
about 1 cup warm water
oil for deep frying
1¼ cups sugar
1 cup water
few drops yellow food coloring
few drops rose water

◆ **Zaffrani chawal**/Saffron rice *(above), a dessert featuring almonds and pistachio nuts — see page 101*

◆ **Phalon ki chaat**/Fruit salad *(right) makes a refreshing snack or starter — see page 100*

◆ **Besan laddu**/Gram flour balls — *see page 100*

TYPICAL MENUS

	★ ★ ★
Rice	
Poori	Matar pillau
Arhar dal	Poori
Rasadar aloo	Sabu bhindi
Kaddu ki sabzi	Shami kabab
Boondi raita	Sukha aloo
South	Raita
Jelebi	Besan laddu

EASTERN INDIA

The section on Eastern India has the largest number of recipes and a special bias towards West Bengal, as this is the region of my birth. The area contains the states of Assam, Orissa and West Bengal, home of India's largest city, Calcutta. It provides a wonderland of many different terrains and just as many cuisines. Within a few hours you can travel from the vast sandy beaches of Orissa to West Bengal, a verdant expanse of paddy fields and rivers, and then east to the endless tea slopes of Assam.

Bengali cooking brings a special art to the kitchen that I have not seen in other parts of India. All regional cooking has its specialities, but I am sure Bengali cooking demands something more. Many Bengali women remember with a mixture of nostalgia and dread their early days as a bride when their mother-in-laws would judge them by their skill at cutting vegetables, fish and meat. New brides move into their parents-in-law's house, and are expected to take over the cooking for their new families. The rules are many; for example, for a tiny fish that must be cooked whole in a gravy, the potatoes must be cut thin, almost like french fries, but inclined more to a half moon shape. As for dicing, you must slice potatoes into small squares for a dry vegetable dish and then quarter them for egg or meat curries. Even fish has to be cut in a particular way, dictated by the recipe, and only specific spices can be used for certain types of dishes.

Bengali food is not ladled onto the plate all at once, but served course by course. You begin with something bitter to clear the palate for the good food to come. This might be Shukto (Bitter vegetable curry) or just fried bitter gourd. Next comes the rice dish served with dal and something fried, say eggplant (quartered or sliced), after which you move on to a dry or gravied vegetable dish. The fish course follows, and, if two kinds of fish are to be served, you eat the lighter one before the richer. Rice is very important, so the rice plate is always restocked and offered around just as wine

glasses are never allowed to stay empty in a good French restaurant. If there is meat on the menu it follows the fish. A homemade sweet and sour chutney follows to clear away the grease from the mouth and prepare for the sweet yogurts and sweetmeats. And finally, a paan—an assortment of spices wrapped in a betelnut leaf—is served to aid digestion.

Wedding feasts are special in many ways. For example, the guests eat not from plates but from banana leaves. Before they are shown to their places—which may be chairs or spaces on the floor— a slice of lime and a little salt is placed on the leaves; these are the condiments. Portions of rice and other courses follow, also served on the leaves.

In West Bengal there is a maze of riverine tracts, fringed with palm trees and banana plantations. The mustard fields that carpet the landscape have given the state its name, Sonar Bangla or Golden Bengal, and the mustard itself is an essential ingredient of Bengali fish cookery.

Bengal used to be much larger, but at the time of the partition it was split into East and West and a segment of it is now in Bangladesh. Bangladesh is similar to Bengal both in cuisine and physical features, but differs in its rich Muslim heritage.

If you were to visit one of the markets you would see a huge variety of fish available, such as the hilsa, pabda, topsey, rui, bekti, chingri and mourala; all of which would probably look strange to you. The hilsa, pure silver in color, is normally eaten between the festivals of Saraswati Puja, for the Goddess of Education, and Kali Puja, for the Goddess of Strength. The topsey, slightly orange at the edges, is usually fried in batter, and the bekti is filleted and used for fried fish or in a curry.

In India, cooking is the privilege of the women, and talking about it the prerogative of the men. Bengalis are immensely fond of good food and spend a lot of time eating it, and discussing it. Moreover, because it features so strongly in their lives, they also spend a significant proportion of their incomes buying the very best food.

Unlike many other communities, Bengalis will eat only with their right hands and can tear Lucchis (Deep fried flour pancakes—*see Breads and Rice for recipe*) expertly with the thumb and their right hands and can tear Lucchis (Deep fried flour pancakes, with the forefinger of one hand, whereas most others use both hands. There are hardly any Bengali restaurants either in India or abroad. This is because they eat the kind of food that loses its entire personality if not served and eaten in the proper Bengali manner.

The basic ingredients for Bengali cooking—rice and fish—are also used in their customs. Rice is sprinkled over individuals as a blessing, for example over a newly married couple or an expectant mother, or on a boy during the thread ceremony, held when he comes of age. Ground rice is mixed to a paste and used to make filigree designs on the floor on festive occasions. Decorated fish is sent to the groom's home from the bride's and vice versa. Fish even plays a part in football matches—not on the field but later. Supporters celebrate their team's victory by sending each other gifts of fish. Mustard oil is used for cooking fish and for certain vegetables, and Bengalis add sugar to most of their cooking be it vegetables, fish or meat.

Orissa is the state of the Sun Temple, Konark, which is renowned for its erotic sculptures. It is a rural state and the land near the coast is fertile and rich in cashew nut trees. Puri, on the coast, is a holy city known for the Jagannath Temple and the Rath Yatra or car festival, which commemorates the journey of Krishna from Gokul to Mathura. The images of Krishna's brother and sister are brought out from the temple and dragged away in huge cars known as raths. The cars are so big that to haul them takes over 4,000 professional car pullers; the English word "juggernaut" derives from this car festival at Jagannath.

Many tribal groups still live in Orissa, and the Khounds are one such group. They used to perform human sacrifices but these were outlawed during the British rule and they have substituted animal sacrifices.

Assam is known for its tea. It lies at the foothills of the Himalayas and has many tropical forests. Of interest to visitors are the wildlife reserves which are home for India's rare, one horned rhinoceros. The people are mainly non-vegetarian and, surprisingly, drink plenty of alcohol.

EASTERN INDIA

SRINAGAR
HIMALAYAS
DELHI
JAIPUR AGRA
GANGES
CALCUTTA
BOMBAY
GOA
MADRAS
INDIAN OCEAN
ARABIAN SEA
SRI LANKA

Cholar Dal

Spicy lentils with coconut

LEGUMES

1 scant cup channa dal, washed
about 6 cups water
1½ tbsp ghee
¾ tsp whole cumin seeds
2 bay leaves
2 dried red chilies
2 in piece of stick cinnamon
4 cardamom pods
¾ tsp ground turmeric
½ tsp chili powder
1¼ tsp ground cumin
1 tsp salt
½ tsp sugar
2 tbsp shredded coconut
1 tbsp raisins

1 In a large saucepan, bring the channa dal and water to a boil over a medium high heat. Throw away the scum.

2 Lower the heat, cover the pan, leaving the lid slightly open, and simmer for about 1¼ hours until soft.

3 Heat the ghee in a small pan over a medium heat. Add the whole cumin seeds, bay leaves, red chilies, cinnamon and cardamom and let them sizzle for a few seconds.

4 Add the turmeric, chili powder, ground cumin, salt and sugar and stir fry for 1 minute. Add the shredded coconut and raisins and fry for another 1–2 minutes.

5 Add the ghee and spices to the hot dal and stir.

Serve with Lucchi and something fried.

Musoor Dal

Simple red lentils

LEGUMES

1 scant cup red lentils
4¼ cups water
¼ tsp ground turmeric
1 tsp salt
3–4 green chilies
1 tbsp oil
2 dried red chilies
½ tsp onion seed
1 tbsp coriander leaves, chopped (optional)

1 Place the lentils, water, turmeric, salt and chilies in a large saucepan and bring to a boil. Throw away the scum.

2 Lower the heat, cover, leaving the lid slightly open, and simmer for about 40 minutes until tender.

3 Using a hand whisk, mix the lentils until smooth (you can also use a food processor).

4 In a small pan, heat the oil until very hot, add the red chilies, and after 2–3 seconds add the onion seed. Let them sizzle for 3–4 seconds.

5 Add the oil with the whole spices to the lentils and bring to a boil once again.

6 Before serving, add the coriander leaves if desired.

Mooror Dal

Lentils cooked with fish heads

1 Dry roast the lentils, stirring constantly, until golden brown.

2 Wash the lentils in several changes of water. Bring the lentils to a boil in the measured amount of water with the turmeric and salt.

3 Throw away the scum, lower heat, cover, leaving the lid slightly open, and simmer for about 1 hour. Put aside.

4 Heat the oil in a pan, and fry the fish heads until golden brown.

5 Drain the fish heads and add to the lentils. Put the remaining oil aside. Bring the lentils to a boil again, add the green chilies, lower heat and simmer for about 15 minutes.

6 In a small pan, heat the remaining oil again until very hot. Add the dried red chilies and fry for 4–5 seconds. Add the onion and stir fry until golden brown.

7 Add the chili powder, cardamom, cinnamon, bay leaves and sugar and fry for a few seconds.

8 Add to the lentils and stir thoroughly.

LEGUMES

1 scant cup moong dal
about 6 cups water
¼ tsp ground turmeric
1 tsp salt
¼ cup oil
2 fish heads, quartered
3 green chilies
2 dried red chilies
1 medium onion, chopped
¼ tsp chili powder
4 cardamom pods
2 in piece of stick cinnamon
2 bay leaves
good pinch of sugar

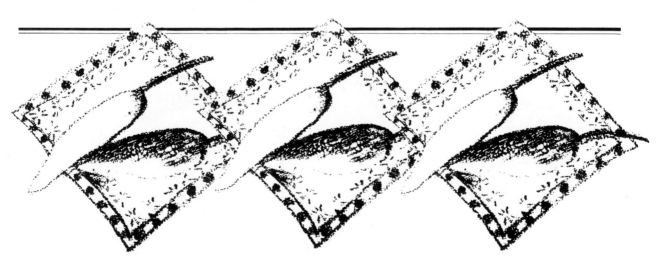

Aloo Peper Dalna

VEGETABLES

Potato and green papaya curry

1 Heat the oil in a karai or a saucepan over a medium high heat.

2 Fry the papaya, a few pieces at a time, until slightly brown. Remove and set aside.

3 Fry the potatoes, a few pieces at a time, until slightly brown. Remove and set aside.

4 Lower heat to medium, add the cumin seeds and bay leaves and let them sizzle for 3–4 seconds. Add the tomatoes and fry for 1–2 minutes.

5 Add the turmeric, chili, cumin, salt and sugar and mix with the tomatoes and fry for a further 1 minute.

6 Add the papaya and potatoes and mix well with the spices. Add the water and bring to a boil. Cover and cook for 15–20 minutes until the vegetables are tender.

7 Add the ghee and the garam masala before removing from the heat.

6 tbsp oil
1 lb/4 cups green papaya, peeled, seeded and cut into 1 in cubes
2½ cups potatoes, peeled and cut into 1 in cubes
1 tsp whole cumin seeds
2 bay leaves
2 tomatoes, chopped
¾ tsp ground turmeric
½ tsp chili powder
1½ tsp ground cumin
¾ tsp salt
large pinch of sugar
1¼ cups water
2 tsp ghee
½ tsp garam masala powder

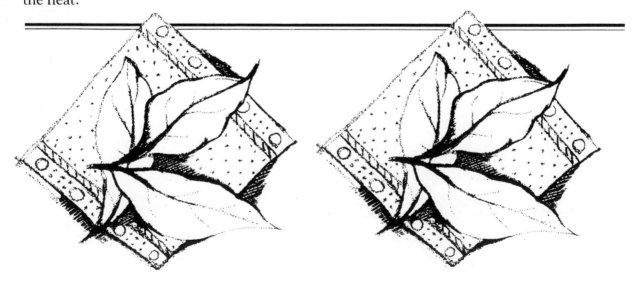

◆ **Musoor dal**/Simple red lentils (*top*) — *see page* 108

Lau Ghonto

VEGETABLES

Dry doddy

1 Heat the oil in a karai or saucepan over a medium high heat. Add the green chilies and let them sizzle for a few seconds. Add the bay leaves and fenugreek. After 3–4 seconds add the doddy and fry for 3–4 minutes, stirring constantly.

2 Add the rest of the ingredients and mix with the doddy.

3 Lower heat, cover and cook for 20–25 minutes, stirring occasionally, so that it does not stick to the base of the pan.

4 Remove the cover, turn the heat up and, stirring constantly, fry until all the liquid has evaporated.

Doddy is a vegetable widely available in supermarkets and in Indian stores, but green papaya may also be used.

3 tbsp oil
2 green chilies, halved
2 bay leaves
1 tsp fenugreek
1½ lb/6 cups doddy, peeled and grated
¾ tsp ground turmeric
½ tsp chili powder
1½ tsp ground cumin
1 tsp salt
¼ tsp sugar

Choch Chori

VEGETABLES

Mixed vegetables

1 Cut the potatoes into 8 pieces lengthwise.

2 Quarter the white radish lengthwise and cut into 1½ in lengths.

3 Cut off the stalk from the eggplant and quarter lengthwise. Cut into 1½ in lengths.

4 Cut the pumpkin into 1 in cubes.

5 Cut the cauliflower stalks into very thin strips of 2½ in long.

6 Heat the oil in a karai or saucepan over a medium high heat, add the dried chilies and fry until they become brownish black (about 4–5 seconds).

7 Add the panch phoron and bay leaves and let them sizzle for a few seconds.

1 medium potato, peeled
1½ cups white radish, scraped
1 small eggplant
1½ cups pumpkin, peeled
2½ cups cauliflower stalks
¼ cup oil
2–3 dried red chilies, broken in half
1 tsp panch phoron
2 bay leaves
¾ tsp ground turmeric
½ tsp chili powder
1½ tsp mustard seeds, ground
1½ tsp salt
½ tsp sugar
½ cup water

8 Add all the vegetables and fry for 3–4 minutes, stirring constantly.

9 Add the turmeric, chili, mustard, salt and sugar and mix thoroughly with the vegetables.

10 Lower heat to medium, cover and cook for 10 minutes.

11 Remove the cover, give the vegetables a good stir and then add the water. Bring to a boil, cover again and cook for about 10–15 minutes, until all the vegetables are tender and all the water has evaporated.

Serve with rice and Musoor dal.

Shukto

Bitter vegetable curry

VEGETABLES

1½ cups white radish, scraped
1 cup potatoes, peeled
1 cup French beans
¾ cup bitter gourd
1 medium green banana, peeled
1 tbsp oil
½ tsp whole mustard seeds
½ in ginger, grated
1 tsp salt
¼ tsp sugar
about 2 cups water

1 Wash all the vegetables.

2 Quarter the white radish lengthwise and then cut into ¼ in slices.

3 Quarter the potatoes lengthwise and then cut into ½ in slices.

4 Cut the beans into 1 in pieces.

5 Cut the bitter gourd into ¼ in slices.

6 The green banana should be halved lengthwise and then cut into ½ in slices.

7 Heat the oil in a karai or saucepan over a medium high heat. Add the mustard seeds and, as soon as they start to splutter, add the ginger and fry for 5–6 seconds.

8 Add all the vegetables, salt and sugar and stir fry for 5–6 minutes.

9 Add the water, bring it to a boil, cover, lower heat and cook until all the vegetables are tender.

◆ **Shukto**/Bitter vegetable curry *(above) is served with rice — see page 113*

◆ **Choch chori**/Mixed vegetables *(right) can be made with any combination of vegetables — see page 112*

Bhape Chingre

Steamed shrimp

1 lb jumbo shrimp
1 tsp ground turmeric
½ tsp chili powder
1 tsp black mustard seeds, ground
2–3 green chilies
1 tsp salt
2 tbsp oil

1 Shell the shrimp, leaving the tails on. Make a small cut down the back to remove the black vein. Wash and pat dry.

2 Thoroughly mix all the ingredients with the shrimp. Place the mixture in a bowl (half fill it only), and tie a double thickness of aluminum foil around the top of the bowl.

3 In a large saucepan, boil some water and place the bowl of shrimp in the saucepan, so that the water reaches a quarter of the way up the bowl.

4 Cover the saucepan, lower the heat and keep boiling, topping up the boiling water during cooking as necessary. Steam for about 30–40 minutes.

◆ **Bhape chingre**/Steamed shrimp

Chingre Macher Malai

SEAFOOD

Shrimp in a coconut sauce

1 lb jumbo shrimp
1½ tsp ground turmeric
1½ tsp salt
⅓ cup creamed coconut
1¼ cups hot water
½ cup oil
2 medium potatoes, peeled and quartered
1 large onion, finely sliced
½ tsp chili powder
½ tsp sugar
2–3 green chilies

1 Shell the shrimp, leaving the tails on. Make a small cut along the back to remove the black vein. Wash and pat dry. Rub ½ tsp each of turmeric and salt into the shrimp.

2 In a food processor or liquidizer, blend together the creamed coconut and water. Put aside.

3 Heat the oil in a saucepan and fry the potatoes until evenly browned. Put aside.

4 Add the shrimp and fry until golden. Put aside.

5 Add the onion to the remaining oil and fry until golden brown. Add the remaining turmeric, salt, chili powder and sugar and fry for 1–2 minutes with the onion.

6 Add the blended coconut milk and bring to a boil. Add the shrimp and green chilies.

7 Cover, lower heat and cook for 10 minutes. Add the potatoes, cover again and cook for a further 20–25 minutes, until the shrimp are cooked and the gravy thickened.

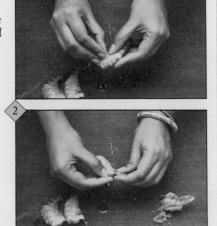

SHELLING SHRIMP
1 *Pinch off the heads with your thumb and forefinger.*
2 *Peel back the body shell from the underside. The whole shell and tail should come away, leaving the flesh intact.*

Elish Macher Paturi

Fish cooked in banana leaves

The burning of the banana leaves adds flavor to this dish.

1 Gently mix the turmeric, chili powder, ground mustard, green chilies, salt and 2 tbsp of oil with the fish.

2 Place 4 banana leaves in a tava or large skillet. Place 1 tbsp of oil on the top leaf and put the pieces of fish in, making sure they do not overlap. Now place the other banana leaves on top. (Grease the leaf in contact with the fish with 1 tbsp of oil.)

3 Cook over a medium heat for 20 minutes. Turn over and cook for a further 20 minutes. (Place a plate over the leaves when you want to turn it over.)

Instead of cooking it on top of the stove, it can be placed on a baking sheet and placed in a preheated oven at 375°F for 30-40 minutes.

1½ lb hilsa (herring), cleaned and cut in 1 in slices
1 tsp ground turmeric
½ tsp chili powder
1 tsp black mustard seeds, ground
2–3 green chilies
1 tsp salt
¼ cup oil
8 banana leaves

Dahi Mach

Fish in a yogurt sauce

1 Sprinkle ½ tsp of salt on the fish and rub into the pieces.

2 Heat the ghee in a karai or saucepan over a medium high heat, and gently fry the pieces of fish, a few at a time, until lightly golden. Put aside.

3 In the remaining ghee, add the cardamom, cinnamon and bay leaves and let them sizzle for 3–4 seconds.

4 Add the onion, ginger and raisins and fry, stirring constantly, until the onion is golden.

5 Add the chilies, yogurt and water mixture, sugar and the remaining salt and bring to a boil. Gently add the pieces of fish. Cover, lower heat and cook for 15–20 minutes until the fish is cooked and the gravy slightly thickened.

1½ lb white fish, cleaned and cut into 1 in pieces
1½ tsp salt
4 tbsp ghee
4 cardamom pods
2 in piece of stick cinnamon
2 bay leaves
1 medium onion, finely sliced
¾ in ginger, grated
1 tbsp raisins
2–3 green chilies
about ½ cup natural yogurt } lightly whisked ¾ cup water } together
½ tsp sugar

◆ **Elish Macher Paturi**/Fish cooked in banana leaves — *see page 116*

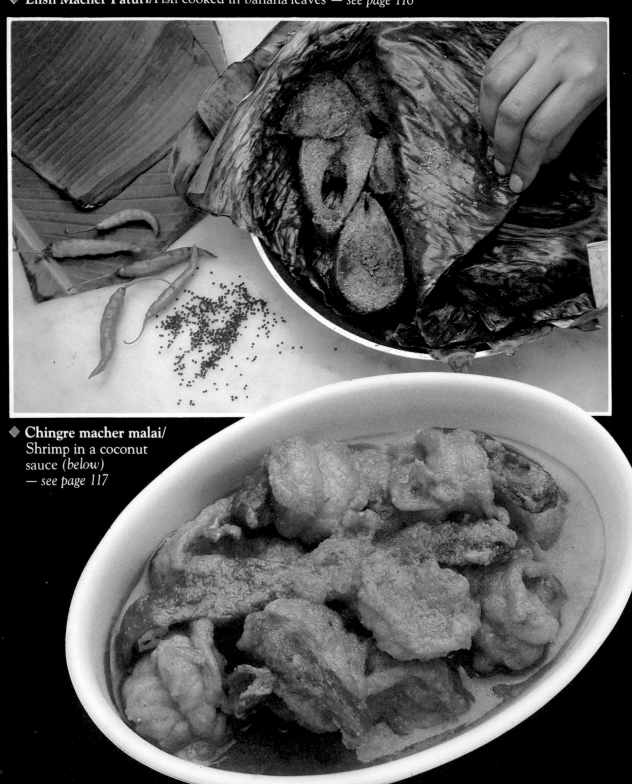

◆ **Chingre macher malai/**
Shrimp in a coconut
sauce *(below)*
— *see page 117*

Macher Jhol

Light fish curry

FISH

1 Cut the fish into 10 equal size pieces. Sprinkle ½ tsp each of turmeric and salt on the fish and rub into the pieces.

2 In a small bowl, mix together the remaining turmeric, salt, chili powder and cumin with the 3 tbsp of water and set aside.

3 In a karai or saucepan, heat the oil over a medium high heat and fry the potatoes until evenly browned. Put aside.

4 In the remaining oil, add the pieces of fish, a few at a time, and fry until light brown in color. Put aside.

5 Add the onion seed and green chilies to the remaining oil and let them sizzle for 3–4 seconds. Add the spices and stir fry for 1–2 minutes.

6 Add the water and bring to a boil; gently add the pieces of fish and potatoes. Cover, lower heat and cook for about 15 minutes until the fish is cooked and the potatoes are tender.

7 Sprinkle with the coriander leaves.

1½ lb rui (or any white fish), cleaned
1¼ tsp ground turmeric
1½ tsp salt
½ tsp chili powder
1 tsp ground cumin
3 tbsp hot water
6 tbsp oil
1 large potato, peeled and cut into 8 pieces
½ tsp onion seed
2–3 green chilies, slit in half
1½ cups water
1 tbsp coriander leaves, chopped

◆ **Macher jhal**/Fish in a hot sauce — *see page 120*

Macher Jhal

FISH

Fish in a hot sauce

1½ lb white fish, cleaned
1½ tsp ground turmeric
1½ tsp salt
½ cup oil
1 large onion, finely sliced
½ tsp chili powder
1 cup water
2–3 green chilies

1 Cut the fish into 8–10 equal size pieces.

2 Rub ½ tsp each of turmeric and salt into the fish.

3 Heat the oil in a karai or saucepan over a medium high heat and fry the pieces of fish, a few at a time, until lightly browned. Put aside.

4 In the remaining oil, fry the onion until brown. Add the remaining turmeric, salt and chili powder and stir fry for a further 1 minute.

5 Add the water and bring to a boil; gently add the pieces of fish and the green chilies. Cover, lower heat to medium and cook for about 15 minutes until the fish is cooked and the gravy thickened.

Muri Ghonto

FISH

Dry fish head curry

6 tbsp oil
2 fish heads, quartered
3 cardamom pods
2 in pieces of stick cinnamon
2 bay leaves
2 medium onions, chopped
¾ in ginger, grated
1 tsp ground turmeric
½ tsp chili powder
1 tsp salt
¼ tsp sugar
1 tbsp raisins (optional)
¼ cup rice, washed and dried
1 cup water

1 Heat the oil in a karai or saucepan over a medium high heat and fry the fish heads until browned. Put aside.

2 In the remaining oil, add the cardamom, cinnamon and bay leaves and let them sizzle for 3–4 seconds. Add the onions and ginger and stir fry until the onions are slightly brown.

3 Add the turmeric, chili, salt, sugar and raisins and, stirring constantly, fry for 1–2 minutes. Add the rice and continue to fry for a further 2 minutes.

4 Add the fish heads and mix with the rice and spices. Add the water and bring to a boil.

5 Cover, lower heat and, stirring occasionally, cook for about 20 minutes until the rice is cooked.

Serve with rice.

Macher Kalia

Fish curry

FISH

1½ lb white fish, cleaned
1½ tsp ground turmeric
1½ tsp salt
1 medium onion, quartered
2 cloves garlic
¾ in ginger
1 tbsp vinegar
8 tbsp oil
2 medium potatoes, peeled and quartered
4 cardamom pods
2 × 1 in pieces of stick cinnamon
2 bay leaves
½ tsp chili powder
¼ tsp sugar
1¼ cups water
3–4 green chilies

1 Cut the fish into 8–10 equal size pieces.

2 Rub ½ tsp each of turmeric and salt into the fish.

3 In a food processor or liquidizer, blend together the onion, garlic, ginger and vinegar.

4 Heat the oil in a karai or saucepan and fry the potatoes, turning often, until evenly browned. Put aside.

5 Gently add a few pieces of fish and fry until golden. Put aside.

6 In the remaining oil, add the cardamom, cinnamon and bay leaves and let them sizzle for 5–6 seconds.

7 Add the blended mixture and, stirring constantly, fry until golden brown.

8 Add the remaining turmeric, salt, chili power and sugar, mix thoroughly with the onion mixture and fry for 1–2 minutes.

9 Add the water and green chilies and bring to a boil. Add the pieces of potato and fish. Cover, lower heat and cook for 15–20 minutes until the potatoes are tender.

Serve with rice.

◇ **Macher kalia**/Fish curry — *see page 121*

Sarshee Mach

Fish with mustard

1 Cut the fish into 8–10 equal size pieces.

2 Rub ½ tsp each of turmeric and salt into the pieces of fish.

3 Mix together the remaining turmeric, salt, chili powder and ground mustard with the 3 tbsp of hot water in a small bowl. Cover with a saucer and set aside for 15–20 minutes for the mustard to become stronger.

4 Heat the oil in a karai or saucepan over a medium high heat, and fry the pieces of fish, a few at a time, until lightly browned. Put aside.

FISH

1½ lb white fish, cleaned
1½ tsp ground turmeric
1½ tsp salt
½ tsp chili powder
1 tsp black mustard seeds, ground
3 tbsp hot water
½ cup oil
½ tsp onion seed
2–3 green chilies, slit in half lengthwise
1 cup water

5 In the remaining oil, add the onion seed and green chilies and let them sizzle for 4–5 seconds. Add the spices and stir fry for 1–2 minutes.

6 Add the water and bring to the boil. Put the pieces of fish in gently. Cover, lower heat to medium and cook for about 15 minutes until the fish is tender and the gravy thickened.

Mangsho Jhol

MEAT

Light meat curry

6 tbsp oil
3 medium potatoes, peeled and halved
4 cardamom pods
2 in piece of stick cinnamon
2 bay leaves
1 large onion, finely sliced
2 cloves garlic, crushed
1 in ginger, grated
1 tsp ground turmeric
½ tsp chili powder
1 tsp salt
good pinch of sugar
1 tbsp vinegar
2 lb/5⅓ cups lamb, cut into 1 in cubes
3¾ cups water

1 Heat the oil in a large saucepan over a medium high heat, and fry the pieces of potato until evenly browned. Put aside.

2 Put the cardamom, cinnamon and bay leaves in the hot oil and let them sizzle for 4–5 seconds. Add the onions, garlic and ginger and fry until the onions are golden brown.

3 Add the turmeric, chili, salt, sugar and vinegar and fry for another minute.

4 Add the lamb, mix with the spices and fry, stirring constantly, for 10–15 minutes until all the meat juices have evaporated.

5 Add the water and bring to a boil. Cover, lower heat and cook for 40 minutes, stirring occasionally.

6 Add the potatoes, cover again and cook for a further 20 minutes until the meat and potatoes are tender.

Serve with rice.

Bhaja

SNACK

Frying

Bhaja means to fry. You can fry a variety of vegetables or fish, and they can be eaten at the beginning of a meal or as a light snack at any time.

Aloo Bhaja

SNACK

Fried potatoes

1 Slice the potatoes thinly and rub in the salt.

3–4 medium potatoes, peeled
½ tsp salt
oil for shallow frying

2 Heat the oil over a high heat and fry the potatoes until golden.

Baigun Bhaja

SNACK

Fried eggplant

1 Slice the eggplant into ½ in thick rounds. Rub with the salt, turmeric and sugar and leave in a sieve for 30 minutes for the excess water to drain out.

1 large eggplant
½ tsp salt
pinch of ground turmeric
pinch of sugar
oil for shallow frying

2 Heat the oil over a medium high heat and fry the eggplant until brown in color, turning once.

Mach Bhaja

SNACK

Fried fish

1 Rub the salt and turmeric into the fish and leave aside for 15–20 minutes.

1 lb medium size herring, cleaned and washed
1 tsp salt
½ tsp ground turmeric
oil for shallow frying

2 Heat the oil over a medium high heat and fry the fish for about 3–4 minutes on each side.

Bengalis eat bhajas with rice and lentils at most meals.

Chop

Spicy ground lamb wrapped with potatoes

Filling

1 Heat the oil in a large skillet over a medium high heat. Add the onion, garlic and ginger and fry for 4–5 minutes, stirring constantly, until the onion becomes pale gold.

2 Add the turmeric, chili, salt, sugar, raisins and vinegar, mix thoroughly with the onion and fry for 1 minute. Add the ground lamb and mix with the spices.

3 Cover, lower heat, and, stirring occasionally, cook for about 20 minutes. Remove the cover, turn the heat up and, stirring constantly, cook until all the liquid has evaporated and the ground lamb is dry.

4 Mix in the garam masala and remove from the heat and set aside to cool.

Chop

1 Mash the potatoes with the cumin, chili and salt. Divide into 20–22 balls.

2 Take a ball and make a depression in the middle with your thumb, to form a cup shape. Fill the center with the ground meat and re-form the potato ball, making sure no cracks appear. Make all the chop in this manner. (The chop can be round and flat or long in shape.)

3 Place the chop in the egg, one at a time, and roll in the breadcrumbs.

4 Heat the oil over a very high heat, in a large skillet and fry the chop until golden brown, turning once (about 1 minute).

Place the Chop in very hot oil. Otherwise it tends to crack.

1 tsp salt
Filling
2 tbsp oil
1 large onion, finely sliced
2 cloves garlic, crushed
1/2 in ginger, grated
3/4 tsp ground turmeric
1/2 tsp chili powder
1 tsp salt
good pinch of sugar
1 tbsp raisins (optional)
2 tsp vinegar
1 lb/2 cups ground lamb
1 tsp ground garam masala
1 egg (slightly beaten)
breadcrumbs
oil for shallow frying
Chop
1 3/4 lb potatoes, peeled and boiled
1 tsp ground, roasted cumin
1/2 tsp ground, roasted, dried red chilies (optional)

MAKING CHOP

1 Add the salt, cumin and chili to the potatoes.
2 Mash the spices into the potatoes by hand.
3 Continue mashing until you have a firm dough.
4 Work the dough into evenly shaped balls.
5 Make a depression in each ball with your thumb.
6 Fill the center of each ball with the ground lamb mixture.
7 Re-form the ball, making sure no cracks appear.
8 Dip each chop into the beaten egg.
9 Roll the egg-coated ball in breadcrumbs.
10 Fry the chop until they are a deep golden brown.

◆ **Chop**/Spicy ground lamb wrapped with potatoes (*top*) — *see page 125*

◆ **Shingara**/Spicy potatoes in pastry (*above*) — *see page 129*

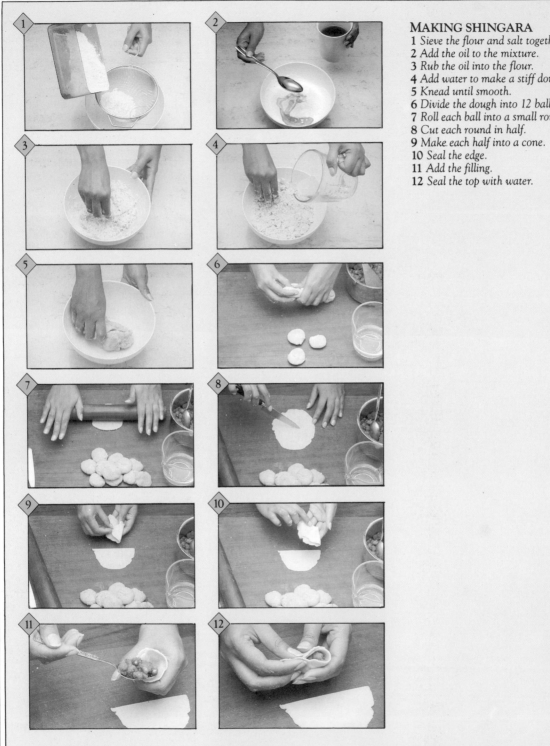

MAKING SHINGARA

1 *Sieve the flour and salt together.*
2 *Add the oil to the mixture.*
3 *Rub the oil into the flour.*
4 *Add water to make a stiff dough.*
5 *Knead until smooth.*
6 *Divide the dough into 12 balls.*
7 *Roll each ball into a small round.*
8 *Cut each round in half.*
9 *Make each half into a cone.*
10 *Seal the edge.*
11 *Add the filling.*
12 *Seal the top with water.*

Shingara

Spicy potatoes in pastry

Filling

1 Heat the oil in a karai or saucepan over a medium high heat and add the cumin seeds. Let them sizzle for a few seconds.

2 Add the potatoes and green chili and fry for 2–3 minutes. Add the turmeric and salt and, stirring occasionally, cook for 5 minutes.

3 Add the peas and the ground roasted cumin. Stir to mix. Cover, lower heat and cook for a further 10 minutes until the potatoes are tender. Cool.

Dough

1 Sieve together the flour and salt. Rub in the oil. Add enough water to form a stiff dough. Knead for 10 minutes until smooth.

2 Divide into 12 balls. Roll each ball into a round of about 6 in across. Cut in half.

3 Pick up one half and form a cone; seal the overlapping edge with a little water. Fill the cone with 1½ tsp of the filling and seal the top with a little water.

4 Make all the shingara in the same way.

5 Heat the oil in a karai or saucepan over a medium heat. Put as many shingara as you can into the hot oil and fry until crisp and golden. Drain.

Serve with a chutney.

Filling
3 tbsp oil
¼ tsp whole cumin seeds
1 lb/4 cups potatoes, diced into ½ in cubes
1 green chili, finely chopped
pinch of turmeric
½ tsp salt
⅓ cup peas
1 tsp ground roasted cumin

Dough
2 cups all-purpose flour
1 tsp salt
3 tbsp oil
about ½ cup hot water
oil for deep frying

Rassogolla

Cheese balls in syrup

2 cups panir, drained
⅔ cup ricotta (or cottage) cheese
1½ cups sugar
about 6 cups water

1 Rub the panir and ricotta cheese with the palms of your hands until smooth and creamy. (This can also be done in a food processor.) Divide into 16 balls.

2 Boil the sugar and water for 5 minutes over a medium heat. Gently put the balls in the syrup and boil for 40 minutes.

3 Cover and continue to boil for another 30 minutes.

Serve warm or cold with a little syrup.

Sandesh

Cheese fudge

2 cups panir, drained
⅓ cup sugar
1 tbsp pistachio nuts, finely chopped

1 Rub the panir with the palms of your hands until smooth and creamy. (Or place in a food processor and process for 20 seconds.)

2 Place the panir in a karai or saucepan over a medium heat, add the sugar and, stirring constantly, cook until it leaves the sides of the pan and forms a ball.

3 Remove from the heat and spread ½ in thick on a plate. Cool slightly, sprinkle with the nuts and cut into small diamonds.

Serve warm or cold.

TYPICAL MENUS

Rice

Shukto

Musoor dal

Aloo peper dalna

Macher jhal

Sandesh

★ ★ ★

Rice

Mooror dal

Choch chori

Sarshee mach

Mangsho jhol

Rassogolla

◆ **Sandesh**/Cheese fudge
(*above right*) *makes the
perfect ending to a meal
— see page 130*

◆ **Rassogolla**/Cheese
balls in syrup *can be
served either warm or
cold — see page 130*

WESTERN INDIA

The region of Western India embraces Gujarat and Maharastra and has many claims to fame. Gujarat is the homeland of the father of modern India, Mahatma Gandhi. It is also the home of many of India's finest vegetarian dishes, and the thalis of western India have no equal. Bombay, one of the largest industrial centres in India, is situated in this region and boasts one of the most famous of Indian dishes, Bombay duck. The Alphonso mango, the most delicious of all mangoes, grows in Maharashtra and is a basic ingredient of many mouth-watering drinks.

Gujarat and Maharashtra form the western part of India. Gujarat is bordered by the Arabian Sea and the coastal strip is very lush and green. Northern Gujarat is desert land, like parts of Rajasthan.

The Jain religion predominates in Gujarat. Jains will not harm other living creatures and their high priests wear gauze masks around the nose and mouth, so that they will not inhale minute insects involuntarily. They are, of course, strict vegetarians and Gujaratis in general have followed suit.

The vegetarian food from here is the best known and the most delicious of all India. Gujaratis are famous for their Dhoklas (Steamed lentil cakes) and Khandvi (Rolled gram flour paste), which can be eaten as snacks with pickles or as accompaniments to the main meal.

Though the thali originated in the south of India, it has become popular here, too. A thali is a circular metallic tray with a half inch rim. On this are placed four or five metal katoris (small bowls). The katoris are filled with dal, two or three vegetable dishes, yogurt and a dessert. The rice is heaped luxuriously in the center and either pooris or chappatis are placed on the side(*see Breads and Rice for recipes*). In addition, there are always one or two pickles (*see Accompaniments for recipes*).

When traveling in India, thalis provide a wonderfully filling meal at very little cost.

Gujarati cooking is simple and uses a lot of buttermilk. Ginger and chilies are ground together to a paste and used in most of the dishes, with freshly grated coconut and coriander leaves as garnishes. Both rice and chappatis are common accompaniments. Sweet breads are also made here, such as Puran poori which is flat bread stuffed with sweetened lentils. Other than Bengalis, Gujaratis are the only people in India who use sugar when cooking savory foods.

Cotton is grown in Gujarat, and, as a result, the region has a rich textile industry. This is the area, too, where Zari, or gold embroidery work, is fashioned by skilled craftsmen, and Gujaratis are also famous for their block printing and tie and dye work, known as Bandhini.

Mahatma Ghandi, the father of modern India, was born in Gujarat and returned to his native region after his years of studying and working abroad. And it was from here that he started the Independence movement against the British after the massacre at Amritsar in 1919.

The state of Maharashtra has the large, industrial city of Bombay as its capital. Bombay is known as the Hollywood of India because it is the home of the Hindi film industry. It also has the busiest port in India, and has been a trading port since the British took over the islands in the mid seventeenth century.

Marathi people are hard working with simple eating habits and good food. Along the Chowpatty Beach you find row upon row of men selling Bhel poori (Savory puffed rice) and Pau bhaji (a simple vegetarian snack) in the evenings. These are wonderfully tasty and really must be savored when walking and enjoying the sea air.

Maharashtra is a large agricultural state and ·most of it lies on the Deccan Plateau. On the coastal side, coconut trees cover the vast expanse of fertile land, and coconuts figure prominently in the Marathis' cooking. Rice and wheat are both eaten here. The vegetarian dishes are similar to the Gujarati dishes except that fish is also eaten here. Pomfret, a flat fish (see Patra ni machi in Foreign Influences), and Bombay duck are from this region.

(Bombay duck, incidentally, is not a duck at all but dried fish, which is usually bought ready prepared.) The people here love fish to such an extent that they store Bombay duck in airtight containers so that they can have the pleasure of eating it all year round. They need to preserve it in this way as absolutely no fishing takes place during the harsh monsoon season.

Another of India's tasty delights is the mango, and the king of mangoes, the Alphonso, grows in Maharashtra. Alphonsos are medium size mangoes with a strong aroma and lovely texture. They can be eaten either chilled or at room temperature. There are various methods of eating mangoes. I suggest peeling the skin off and then slicing the flesh onto a plate. Some flesh will adhere to the large stone, and to eat this you will have to put your dignity aside and simply bite into the flesh, holding the stone in your hands; these mangoes are much too good to waste. During the summer months, when mangoes are in season, chilled mango juice is a favorite drink. Sometimes milk and nuts are added. You can make your own version by adding milk and sugar to canned mango pulp. It is like a rich and delicious milkshake.

The world famous Ajanta and Ellora cave temples are in Maharashtra. Ajanta is renowned for its paintings, all of which are Buddhist, while Ellora is famous for its sculptures. Built later than the Ajanta, when Buddhism was in a period of decline, these cave temples were predominantly Hindu and Jain.

At the time of the partition of India, Hindus from Sind, which is now in Pakistan, came and settled in India. Most of them have made their homes in Bombay. They have their own distinct cuisine and are mainly non-vegetarians. Elaichi gosht (Lamb with cardamom) is one of their specialties, and you can find the recipe in this section.

Aamti

Spicy lentils

1 Place the toovar dal, water, turmeric and salt in a large saucepan and bring to a boil.

2 Cover, leaving the lid slightly open, and simmer the dal for about 40–45 minutes until tender. In a food processor or liquidizer, blend the dal until smooth; return to the saucepan.

3 Heat the oil in a small saucepan. Add the mustard seeds, garlic and cumin seeds and fry until the mustard seeds start to splutter.

4 Add the tamarind juice and bring to a boil, stirring constantly. Add this to the dal and mix thoroughly. Boil for 5 minutes.

5 Garnish with the coriander leaves and serve hot.

LEGUMES

½ cup toovar dal, washed
3¾ cups water
pinch of turmeric
1 tsp salt
1 tbsp oil
½ tsp mustard seeds
1 clove garlic, crushed
½ tsp whole cumin seeds
½ cup tamarind juice
2 tbsp coriander leaves, chopped

Dal Dhokri

Lentils with spicy dumplings

1 Grind the chilies and ginger together into a paste.

2 Place the toovar dal, water, turmeric, salt, and chili and ginger paste in a large saucepan and bring to the boil. Cover, leaving the lid slightly open, and simmer for 40–45 minutes until the dal is tender. Add the sugar and lime juice and mix thoroughly. Remove from the heat and put aside.

Dough

1 Sieve together the wholewheat flour, gram flour, chili powder, turmeric, asafetida and salt.

2 Rub in the oil.

3 Add enough water to make a stiff dough. Knead for 8–10 minutes until soft and smooth.

4 Divide into 4 portions. Take one, flatten slightly and roll

LEGUMES

2 green chilies
½ in ginger
1 scant cup toovar dal, washed
3¾ cups water
½ tsp ground turmeric
1 tsp salt
½ tsp sugar
2–3 tbsp lime juice
Dough
1 cup wholewheat flour
1 tbsp gram flour
½ tsp chili powder
pinch of turmeric
pinch of asafetida
½ tsp salt
1 tbsp oil
about ¼ cup hot water
1 tbsp ghee

into a round 8 in across. Cut into small diamond shapes; do the same with the other portions.

5 In a small saucepan, heat the oil, add the mustard and cumin seeds and, as soon as the seeds start to splutter, add the asafetida and cinnamon and fry for 2–3 seconds. Add to the dal.

6 Add the small diamond pieces of dough to the dal, bring to a boil again and boil for 12–15 minutes, stirring occasionally. (Add a little water if the dal gets too thick.)

7 Garnish with the coconut, coriander and ghee.

Serve hot—this is a meal by itself.

½ tsp mustard seeds
½ tsp whole cumin seeds
pinch of asafetida
good pinch of cinnamon
2 tbsp coconut, grated
2 tbsp coriander leaves, chopped
2 tbsp ghee

Khatta Moong

LEGUMES

Soured lentils

1 Wash the dal thoroughly. Place the dal, 2½ cups of water, pinch of turmeric and ½ tsp salt in a saucepan and bring to a boil. Lower the heat, cover, leaving the lid slightly open, and simmer until the dal has split open, but is still whole. (It should not become mushy.) Drain and put aside.

2 Whisk together the yogurt, water and gram flour until smooth.

3 Grind 2 green chilies and the ginger to a paste.

4 Heat the ghee in a large saucepan. Add 2 green chilies, broken in half, cinnamon, cumin and asafetida and let them sizzle for 5–6 seconds.

5 Add the yogurt mixture, the remaining turmeric and salt, sugar and the chili and ginger paste. Stirring constantly, cook for 5–7 minutes.

6 Add the drained dal and cook for a further 5 minutes until thick. Garnish with the coriander leaves.

The yogurt should be left at room temperature for 24 hours so that it has a slightly sour taste.

½ cup whole moong dal
2½ cups water
½ tsp ground turmeric
1 tsp salt
½ cup yogurt
3 cups water
2 tbsp gram flour
4 green chilies
½ in ginger
2 tsp ghee
1 in piece of stick cinnamon
½ tsp cumin seeds
pinch of asafetida
½ tsp sugar
2 tbsp coriander leaves, chopped

Aloo Shak

Dry potatoes

1½ lb potatoes, peeled
3 tbsp oil
1 tsp mustard seeds
½ tsp ground turmeric
½ tsp chili powder
1 tsp salt
2 tbsp coriander leaves, chopped

1 Dice the potatoes into ½ in cubes and boil. Drain.

2 In a saucepan, heat the oil over a medium high heat, add the mustard seeds and let them sizzle for 5–6 seconds.

3 Add the potatoes, turmeric, chili and salt and mix gently.

4 Lower heat to medium and, stirring constantly, cook for about 8–10 minutes.

5 Garnish with coriander leaves.

Serve with Poori.

◆ *The vegetable market in Margoa, the main town of southern Goa*

Aloo Bhaji

Fried potatoes

1 Dice the potatoes into ½ in cubes.

2 Grind 2 green chilies and the ginger to a paste. Cut the other 2 chilies in half, lengthwise.

3 Heat the oil in a skillet over a medium high heat. Add the cinnamon, cumin, mustard, asafetida and the green chilies and, when the mustard starts to splutter, add the potatoes, turmeric, chili, coriander, cumin, salt and the chili and ginger paste. Stir fry for about 5–7 minutes.

4 Add the coriander leaves, and mix well.

Serve hot with Poori.

VEGETABLES

1½ lb potatoes, peeled and boiled
4 green chilies
½ in ginger
2 tbsp oil
1 in piece of stick cinnamon
½ tsp cumin seeds
½ tsp mustard seeds
pinch of asafetida
½ tsp ground turmeric
1 tsp chili powder
1 tsp ground coriander
1 tsp ground cumin
1 tsp salt
1 tbsp coriander leaves, chopped

Besan Curry

Gram flour curry

1 Cut the beans into 2 in lengths.

2 Cut the potatoes into 1 in cubes.

3 Heat the oil in a large saucepan over a medium heat. Add the cumin, asafetida, fenugreek, and ginger and fry for 5–6 seconds.

4 Add the gram flour and, stirring constantly, fry for 3–4 minutes.

5 Add the water, turmeric and salt and boil for 2–3 minutes.

6 Add the vegetables and cook until they are tender.

7 Add the coriander leaves, tamarind juice and sugar and boil for a further 1 minute.

You can add other vegetables like carrots or cauliflower. Always cut the vegetables into large pieces.

VEGETABLES

½ cup French beans, washed
½ lb potatoes, washed
2 tbsp oil
½ tsp whole cumin seeds
pinch of asafetida
¼ tsp fenugreek seeds
½ in ginger, grated
3 tbsp gram flour
2½ cups water
¾ tsp ground turmeric
1 tsp salt
1 tbsp coriander leaves, chopped
about ⅓ cup thick tamarind juice
¼ tsp sugar

Bharaleli Wangi

Stuffed eggplant

VEGETABLES

3 tbsp coconut
ghee for shallow frying
1 tsp coriander seeds
1 tsp cumin seeds
½ tsp sesame seeds
about ¼ cup thick tamarind juice
1 tsp chili powder
1 tsp brown sugar
1 tsp salt
4 long eggplant, washed and dried

1 Chop the coconut coarsely.

2 Heat the ghee and fry the coconut until golden. Drain on paper toweling and put to one side.

3 In a small saucepan, dry roast the coriander, cumin and sesame seeds over a medium heat, stirring constantly, until they turn a few shades darker and emit a lovely aroma.

4 Grind the roasted spices and fried coconut to a fine powder.

5 Mix this powder with the tamarind juice, chili powder, sugar and salt and put aside.

6 Cut off the tops of the eggplant and make two cuts like a cross coming about three-quarters of the way down the length. (Make sure you do not cut right through.)

7 Stuff the spicy mixture into the eggplant.

8 In a large skillet, heat the ghee and fry the eggplant over a gentle heat, turning them from time to time. (Add any remaining spicy mixture to the eggplant while frying.)

Karela

Stuffed bitter gourd

VEGETABLES

1 lb bitter gourds
2–3 tsp salt
½ lb/2 cups potatoes, peeled and diced
¾ cup peas
6 tbsp oil
¼ in ginger, grated
2 cloves garlic, crushed
1 large onion, finely chopped
2–3 green chilies, chopped
2 tbsp coconut, grated
1 tbsp coriander leaves, chopped

1 Peel the bitter gourds and slit them lengthwise along one side. Carefully remove the seeds and pulp. Wash the gourds and sprinkle on 2 tsp of the salt and leave them in a sieve for 3–4 hours to get rid of the bitter taste.

2 Boil the potatoes and peas.

3 Heat 2 tbsp of the oil in a saucepan. Add the ginger, garlic and onion and fry until the onion is lightly golden.

4 Add the chilies, boiled vegetables and ¾ tsp salt and stir fry with the onion for 1 minute.

5 Remove from the heat and mix in the coconut and coriander leaves. Cool.

6 Wash the bitter gourds once again and dry thoroughly. Stuff them carefully with the vegetable mixture. Secure with toothpicks.

7 Heat the remaining oil in a large skillet. Add the stuffed bitter gourds carefully, and fry for 4–5 minutes, stirring occasionally. Cover, lower the heat and cook for about 15 minutes until tender.

Bitter gourd is a vegetable widely available in supermarkets and in Indian stores.

Sai Bhaji

Spinach with lentils and vegetables

¼ cup channa dal, washed
2½ cups water
3 tbsp oil
1 medium onion, finely chopped
½ in ginger, grated
2 cloves garlic, crushed
1 rounded cup spinach, washed and chopped
1 medium potato, diced into ½ in cubes
3 tomatoes, chopped
¼ cup peas
½ tsp ground turmeric
½ tsp chili powder
1 tsp ground coriander
¾ tsp salt

1 Add the channa dal to the measured amount of water, and bring to a boil over a high heat. Cover and simmer for about 40 minutes until the dal is tender. Drain and save the liquid; make this liquid up to 1½ cups with extra water if necessary.

2 Heat the oil in a large saucepan over a medium high heat and fry the onion, ginger and garlic until soft.

3 Add the rest of the ingredients and the boiled dal and, stirring constantly, fry for 2–3 minutes. Add the liquid, bring it to a boil, cover, lower heat to medium low and cook for about 30 minutes.

4 Mash up the vegetables with a wooden spoon.

Serve with Khichuri.

Khara Bhat

Vegetables with rice

1 cup basmati rice
4 tbsp oil
2 green chilies, cut in half lengthwise
1 in piece of stick cinnamon
½ tsp cumin seeds

1 Wash the rice in several changes of water and leave in a sieve to drain.

2 Heat the oil in a large saucepan over a medium high heat.

Add the green chilies, cinnamon, cumin and asafetida and let them sizzle for 5–6 seconds.

3 Add the potatoes and, stirring occasionally, fry until lightly golden all over.

4 Add the onions and fry for 1–2 minutes. Add the eggplant and fry for a further 1 minute.

5 Add the drained rice, garam masala powder, chili powder, turmeric and salt and, stirring constantly, fry for 5–6 minutes.

6 Add the water, bring it to a boil, lower heat to very low, cover and cook for about 20 minutes until all the water has evaporated and the rice and vegetables are tender.

7 Fluff with a fork and serve hot.

pinch of asafetida
2 medium potatoes, peeled and quartered
2 medium onions, peeled and quartered
1 small eggplant, cut into large pieces
¼ tsp garam masala powder
½ tsp chili powder
½ tsp ground turmeric
1 tsp salt
2¼ cups water

Sukhi Sabzi

VEGETABLES

Dry vegetables

1 Heat the oil in a karai or saucepan over a medium heat, add the mustard seeds, asafetida and curry leaves and let them sizzle for 3–4 seconds.

2 Add the potatoes and capsicum and stir fry for 5 minutes.

3 Add the coconut and salt and, stirring occasionally, cook for another 5–7 minutes.

4 Before removing from the heat, sprinkle with the chilies and coriander leaves.

Serve hot with Poori.

1 lb/4 cups potatoes, peeled, boiled and diced into ½ in cubes
3 tbsp oil
½ tsp whole mustard seeds
pinch of asafetida
6–8 curry leaves
1 capsicum (or green pepper), seeded and cut into ½ in pieces
3 tbsp desiccated coconut
½ tsp salt
2 green chilies, chopped
1 tbsp coriander leaves, chopped

Usal

VEGETABLES

Savory bean sprouts

1 Grind together the cumin, turmeric, garlic and chili powder to a fine paste.

2 Heat the oil and fry the onion until golden brown. Add the

¼ tsp cumin seeds
¼ tsp ground turmeric
3 cloves garlic
½ tsp chili powder
3 tbsp oil

◆ **Usal**/Savory bean sprouts
(left) — see page 142

◆ *Vegetables must be in perfect
condition to be acceptable to
the Indian cook (below)*

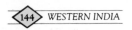

ground paste and fry with the onion for 1 minute.

3 Add the bean sprouts and salt and mix with the spices and stir fry for 2–3 minutes. Add the lime juice.

4 Cover and cook on a low heat for about another 2–3 minutes.

5 Garnish with the coriander leaves and serve hot.

1 medium onion, finely chopped
1 lb/6 cups bean sprouts
1 tsp salt
1 tbsp lime juice
2 tbsp coriander leaves, chopped

Sambharia

Stuffed vegetables

1 Wash the vegetables and dry thoroughly.

2 Cut the eggplant into 1½ in slices.

3 Make 2 cuts crosswise on each vegetable; cut about three quarters of the way down the length, but do not cut right through.

4 Grind together 2 green chilies and the ginger to a paste.

5 Make a paste by mixing the gram flour, coriander, cumin, turmeric, salt, sugar, 2½ tbsp oil, lime juice and the chili and ginger paste.

6 Carefully open the slits in the vegetables and stuff them with this paste. If you have any paste left over after stuffing the vegetables, add it to the vegetables while they are being fried.

7 In a large, heavy based skillet, heat the remaining oil, add 3 green chilies, broken in half, mustard and asafetida and let them sizzle for 8–10 seconds.

8 Add the vegetables carefully, cover and fry over a low heat, occasionally stirring gently. When one side is done, turn the vegetables over, and cover and cook the second side. Add a little more oil if necessary.

Serve hot, garnished with the coconut and coriander.

VEGETABLES

2 long eggplant
6 small potatoes, peeled
6 small onions, peeled
5 green chilies
½ in ginger
¾ cup gram flour
1 tbsp ground coriander
½ tsp ground cumin
pinch of ground turmeric
1 tsp salt
¾ tsp sugar
about ½ cup oil
2 tbsp lime juice
¾ tsp mustard seeds
good pinch of asafetida
2 tbsp coconut, grated
2 tbsp coriander leaves, chopped

Jhinge Batana

Spiced shrimp

SEAFOOD

1 Shell the shrimp, leaving the tails on. Make a small cut along the back to remove the black vein. Wash the shrimp and rub in ½ tsp of the salt and turmeric. Put aside for 1 hour.

2 Grind the garlic, ginger and green chilies to a paste.

3 In a large saucepan, heat the oil and fry the onions until lightly golden.

4 Add the shrimp and paste and stir fry for 2–3 minutes.

5 Add the coriander, cumin and remaining salt, and continue to fry for a further minute.

6 Add the water, bring to a boil, reduce heat to medium low, cover and simmer for 10 minutes.

7 Add the peas, molasses or sugar and tamarind juice, cover again and cook for about 20 minutes until the shrimp are tender. Garnish with the coriander leaves and coconut.

1 lb shrimp
1½ tsp salt
½ tsp ground turmeric
4 cloves garlic
¾ in ginger
4 green chilies
6 tbsp oil
2 medium onions, finely chopped
1½ tsp ground coriander
1½ tsp ground cumin
¾ cup water
1 cup peas
1 tsp molasses or brown sugar
2 tbsp tamarind juice
2 tbsp coriander leaves, chopped
2 tbsp grated coconut

Elaichi Gosht

Lamb with cardamom

MEAT

1 Grind the peppercorns and cardamom seeds finely.

2 In a liquidizer or processor, blend the tomatoes and ginger.

3 Heat the oil in a saucepan and fry the onions until golden. Add the meat and the ground spices. Stir constantly and fry for 5 minutes

4 Add the blended mixture, paprika and salt, mix with the meat and fry for a further 2–3 minutes.

5 Add the water, bring it to a boil, cover, lower heat to very low and cook for about 1 hour until tender.

Garnish with coriander leaves and serve with rice.

30 black peppercorns
25 cardamom pods, skinned
5 medium tomatoes
1 in ginger, cut into small pieces
½ cup oil
2 large onions, finely chopped
2 lb/5⅓ cups lamb, cut into 1 in cubes
2 tsp paprika
1½ tsp salt
1 cup water
3 tbsp coriander leaves, chopped

◆ **Jhinge batana**/Spiced shrimp
*(above) are garnished with coriander
leaves and coconut — see page 145*

◆ **Elaichi gosht**/Lamb with
cardamom *is highly spiced
with peppercorns, cardamom
and ginger —see page 145*

◆ **Bhel poori**/*Savory puffed rice is served with Tamarind chutney and Green chutney*

Batata Poha

Spicy pounded rice

1 Wash the pounded rice and leave to drain in a sieve for about 15 minutes.

2 Heat the oil over a medium high heat and add the mustard seeds; as soon as they start to splutter add the red chilies, green chilies and curry leaves and let them sizzle for 7–8 seconds.

3 Add the onion and stir fry until golden.

4 Add the potatoes, turmeric, salt and chili powder and mix with the onions.

5 Add the drained pounded rice and mix with the other ingredients; stir fry for 2–3 minutes.

6 Lower the heat, cover and cook for about 8–10 minutes, stirring occasionally (add a little extra oil if you think necessary).

7 Sprinkle on the lime juice and coriander leaves. Mix well and serve immediately.

This is eaten for breakfast or as a light snack.

⅔ cup pounded rice
2 tbsp oil
½ tsp mustard seeds
1–2 dried red chilies, broken in half
1–2 green chilies, chopped
5–6 curry leaves
1 small onion, finely chopped
2 medium potatoes, boiled and diced into ½ in cubes
¼ tsp ground turmeric
1 tsp salt
½ tsp chili powder
2 tbsp coriander leaves, chopped

Bhel Poori

Savory puffed rice

1 Mix together the puffed rice, sev, potato, onion, coriander leaves and salt and put aside.

2 Make the tamarind chutney by mixing together the tamarind juice, salt, chili powder and sugar; put aside.

3 Make the green chutney by first chopping the coriander leaves and throwing away the lower stalks and roots.

4 Blend together the coriander leaves, green chilies, salt and lemon juice until smooth. Add a little water if necessary. This sauce should not be too thick.

3¾ cups puffed rice
⅓ cup sev
1 medium potato, boiled and diced into ¼ in cubes
1 small onion, finely chopped
2 tbsp coriander leaves, chopped
½ tsp salt
Tamarind chutney
about ½ cup thick tamarind juice
½ tsp salt
½ tsp chili powder
1½ tsp sugar

5 When you are ready to serve Bhel poori, add the chutneys to the puffed rice mixture (the amount can vary to suit individual taste).

Sev can be bought easily at any Indian grocery store.

Serve immediately as a snack.

Green chutney

4 sprigs of coriander, washed
2 green chilies
½ tsp salt
2–3 tbsp lemon juice
a little water

Bhakhar Vadi

SNACK

Wholewheat pastry with potato stuffing

1 Finely grate the potatoes and soak in water for about 30 minutes. Drain and dry thoroughly.

2 Grind the green chilies and ginger to a paste.

3 Heat 2 tbsp of the oil over a medium high heat. Add the mustard, asafetida and red chilies and let them sizzle for 8–10 seconds.

4 Add the dried potatoes, chili powder, turmeric, 1 tsp salt and the chili and ginger paste and stir fry for 5–7 minutes.

5 Lower the heat slightly, cover and, stirring occasionally, cook for about 25–30 minutes until the potatoes are tender. Add the mango powder and sugar, and mix. Remove from the heat, cool and divide into 4 parts.

6 Sieve together the wholewheat flour, plain flour and 1 tsp salt. Rub in 1 tbsp of oil.

7 Add enough water to make a stiff dough. Knead for 7–10 minutes to make the dough soft and pliable. Divide into 4 portions.

8 Take a portion and roll into an 8 in round on a lightly floured surface. Spread a portion of the potato mixture evenly on the rolled dough. Starting at the side closest to you, carefully roll it up tightly like a jelly roll. Cut into ½ in thick slices. Gently flatten each slice between the palms of your hands.

1½ lb potatoes, washed and peeled
2 green chilies
½ in ginger
3 tbsp oil
½ tsp mustard seeds
pinch of asafetida
2 dried red chilies
¼ tsp chili powder
pinch of ground turmeric
2 tsp salt
1½ tsp mango powder
½ tsp sugar
1 cup wholewheat flour
½ cup plain flour
about ⅓ cup warm water
oil for deep frying

Dhokla/Steamed lentil cakes — *see page 152*

◆ **Khandvi**/Rolled gram
flour paste *(right)* is
served as a snack
— see page 153

◆ **Karhi**/Yogurt curry *(above)*
contains deep-fried Pakoras
and is served with rice
— see page 152

9 Heat the oil for deep frying and carefully fry them for 3–4 minutes until they are golden; turn once.

These can be eaten as a snack or as an accompaniment to a main meal.

Dhokla

Steamed lentil cakes

1 scant cup channa dal
¼ cup water
3 green chilies
½ in ginger
1 tsp salt
pinch of turmeric
¾ tsp baking soda
juice of 1 lime
1 tbsp oil
½ tsp mustard seeds
pinch of asafetida
1 tbsp coconut, grated
1 tbsp coriander leaves, chopped

1 Soak the channa dal overnight in plenty of cold water. The next morning, wash the dal 2 or 3 times.

2 Place the dal and the water in a food processor or blender and blend until smooth.

3 Grind the chilies and ginger together to a paste.

4 Add the chili and ginger paste, salt, turmeric, soda and lime juice to the blended dal and mix thoroughly.

5 Pour the mixture into a greased thali or a shallow cake pan, making sure that it does not come more than three quarters of the way up.

6 Place the thali in a steamer, cover and steam for 20 minutes. Remove from the heat and set aside for 5 minutes. Insert a skewer into the middle to test whether the dhoklas are cooked.

7 Cut into 1½ in squares and arrange on a plate.

8 Heat the oil in a small saucepan, and add the mustard seeds; when they start to splutter, add the asafetida and, after 2–3 seconds, pour this over the cut dhoklas.

9 Garnish with the coconut and coriander leaves.

Karhi

Yogurt curry

Pakoras

1 Make a thick batter with the gram flour, salt, turmeric and water.

Pakoras
½ cup gram flour
¼ tsp salt
pinch of ground turmeric

2 Heat the oil over a medium high heat, drop in a teaspoonful of the batter and fry until crisp and golden. Drain and set aside.

Curry
1 Whisk the yogurt, water and gram flour until smooth.

2 Place the fried pakoras in a bowl of water for 3–4 minutes. Gently squeeze out as much water as possible and put aside.

3 Heat 1 tbsp oil in a large saucepan over a medium heat. Add the fenugreek, asafetida, curry leaves and green chilies and let them sizzle for about 10 seconds.

4 Add the yogurt mixture, turmeric, chili and salt and slowly bring to a boil.

5 Lower the heat, add the pakoras and simmer for about 10 minutes until the sauce has thickened.

Serve hot with rice.

about ¼ cup water
oil for deep frying
Curry
1 cup yogurt
1½ cups water
1 tbsp gram flour
1 tbsp oil
¼ tsp fenugreek seeds
pinch of asafetida
6–8 curry leaves
2 green chilies, chopped
½ tsp ground turmeric
½ tsp chili powder
½ tsp salt

Khandvi

SNACK

Rolled gram flour paste

1 Sieve the gram flour into a large bowl.

2 Lightly beat the yogurt and water together.

3 Grind the chilies and ginger together to make a paste.

4 Add the yogurt and water mixture and the paste to the gram flour and whisk until smooth. Stir in the turmeric and salt. Put the mixture to one side for 1 hour.

5 Pour the mixture into a saucepan and heat gently, stirring constantly until it thickens. (Be careful to let no lumps form.)

6 When the mixture thickens, spread a little thinly on a greased plate and let it cool. Try to roll it; if you cannot, thicken the mixture a little more.

7 Grease 2 or 3 large plates and spread the mixture very thinly on them with the back of a spatula. Allow the mixture to cool.

¾ cup gram flour
4 tbsp yogurt
1½ cups water
2 green chilies
½ in ginger
pinch of ground turmeric
¾ tsp salt
1 tbsp oil
½ tsp mustard seeds
pinch of asafetida
2 tbsp coconut, grated
2 tbsp coriander leaves, chopped

◆ **Masale bhat**/Spiced rice (*above*) is served hot
with ghee — *see page 157*

◆ **Saboodana ki khichiri**/Spicy sago *(above)*
makes a tasty snack — see page 156

8 Cut into ¼ in long strips, and, starting at one end of each strip, roll them up. Place these rolls in a flat serving dish, one next to the other.

9 Heat the oil until very hot. Add the mustard seeds and asafetida and let them sizzle for 8–10 seconds. Pour this over the rolled Khandvi and garnish with the coconut and coriander leaves.

The yogurt should be left at room temperature for about 24 hours so that it acquires a slightly sour taste.

Dal Vada

SNACK

Fried lentil balls

1 Soak the urid dal in plenty of cold water overnight. Drain.

2 In a liquidizer or food processor, blend the dal with all the other ingredients. Add a little water, if necessary, to make a fine, thick paste.

3 Heat the oil over a medium high heat. Drop in a teaspoonful of the mixture and fry until nicely golden.

Serve with a chutney as a snack or as an accompaniment to a main meal.

1 scant cup urid dal, washed
5–6 curry leaves
2–3 green chilies
pinch of asafetida
½ in ginger, grated
¾ tsp cumin seeds
1 tsp salt
oil for deep frying

Saboodana Ki Khichiri

SNACK

Spicy sago

1 Wash the sago and soak in a little water for about 10 minutes. Drain and dry on paper toweling.

2 Roast the peanuts and grind coarsely.

3 Mix the sago and peanuts.

4 Heat the oil in a saucepan over a medium high heat. Add the mustard seeds and green chilies; when the mustard seeds start to splutter, add the asafetida and fry for 2–3 seconds.

5 Add the sago and peanut mixture, turmeric, salt and sugar

1 cup sago
½ cup peanuts, skinned
2 tbsp oil
1 tsp mustard seeds
2 green chilies, chopped
pinch of asafetida
good pinch of turmeric
1 tsp salt
1 tsp sugar
about ⅓ cup water
juice of ½ a lime
1 tbsp coconut, grated
1 tbsp coriander leaves, chopped

and stir fry for 1 minute.

6 Lower the heat and continue to stir fry for another 2–3 minutes.

7 Add the water, cover and cook, stirring occasionally, until the sago is tender and nearly dry.

8 Add the lime juice and give it a good stir.

Serve garnished with coconut and coriander leaves.

Masale Bhat

Spiced rice

RICE

1½ cups basmati rice
3 tsp coriander seeds
2 tsp cumin seeds
½ in piece of stick cinnamon
3 cardamom pods, shelled
2 cloves
3 tbsp oil
¾ tsp mustard seeds
good pinch of asafetida
½ tsp ground turmeric
1 tsp chili powder
1 small cauliflower, broken into large florets
3 cups water
1½ tsp salt
3 tbsp coriander leaves, chopped
3 tbsp coconut, grated

1 Wash the rice in several changes of water and soak for 1 hour in plenty of water. Drain the rice and leave in a sieve for about 20 minutes.

2 While the rice is soaking, dry roast the coriander, cumin, cinnamon, cardamom and cloves over a medium heat, until they are a few shades darker and emit a rich aroma.

3 Grind the spices to a fine powder and put aside.

4 In a large saucepan, heat the oil, add the mustard seeds and let them sizzle for 5–6 seconds. Add the asafetida, turmeric, chili powder and cauliflower and, taking care not to burn the spices, stir fry for 1–2 minutes.

5 Add the rice and sauté for a few minutes, making sure that the rice does not become brown.

6 Add the water, bring it to a boil, give it a good stir, lower the heat to very low, cover and cook for 8 minutes. Remove the cover, add the powdered spices and salt, mix, cover again and cook for a further 10 minutes until all the water is absorbed.

7 Fluff gently with a fork. Garnish with the coriander leaves and coconut.

Serve hot with ghee.

Khichiri

Rice with a few lentils

1 Mix the rice and moong dal and soak in plenty of water for 1 hour. Drain.

2 Add the rice and dal mixture to the measured amount of water in a large saucepan and bring to a boil over a high heat. Lower heat to very low, cover and cook for about 20 minutes until all the water has been absorbed. Remove from the heat.

3 In a small pan, heat the ghee until very hot and pour it over the cooked rice and dal. Mix gently.

Serve hot with Sag bhaji, yogurt and Pappadoms.

1 cup basmati rice, washed
¼ cup moong dal, washed
3 cups water
1½ tbsp ghee

Khamang Kakadi

Cucumber salad

1 Dry roast the peanuts and grind them to a fine powder.

2 Gently squeeze the cucumber to get rid of the excess water.

3 Place the cucumber, coconut, ground peanuts, lemon juice and salt in a bowl and mix gently.

4 In a small saucepan, heat the ghee. Add the cumin seeds and let them sizzle for 3–4 seconds. Add the asafetida and the green chilies and fry for 5–6 seconds. Pour this over the cucumber mixture and mix well.

5 Garnish with the coriander leaves.

2 tbsp unsalted peanuts
½ cucumber, peeled and cut into fine strips
2 tbsp grated coconut
2 tbsp lemon juice
½ tsp salt
1 tbsp melted ghee
¼ tsp cumin seeds
pinch of asafetida
2 green chilies, chopped
1 tbsp coriander leaves, chopped

Kacha Pakka Kobi

Cabbage salad

1 Cut the cabbage very finely into long strips. Wash and dry them.

2 Heat the oil in a large saucepan over a medium high heat.

1 lb green cabbage
1 tsp oil
2 green chilies, chopped
2 tsp urid dal
½ tsp mustard seeds

◆ **Khamang kakadi**/Cucumber salad *(above) has a delicious nutty flavor* — see page 158

◆ *Ground cardamom (left) is widely used in Indian cuisine*

Add the chilies and fry for 3–4 seconds.

3 Remove the pan from the heat, add the urid dal and stir fry until lightly golden (this will take a few seconds only).

4 Put the pan back on the heat and add the mustard seeds; after 8–10 seconds add the asafetida and fry for 2–3 seconds.

5 Add the cabbage and salt and, stirring constantly, cook for 3–4 minutes.

Serve garnished with the coconut and coriander leaves.

pinch of asafetida
¾ tsp coconut, grated
1 tbsp coriander leaves, chopped

Puran Poori

DESSERT

Flat bread stuffed with sweetened lentils

Filling
1 Wash the channa dal in several changes of water.

2 In a large saucepan, bring the dal and water to a boil over a medium high heat. Lower the heat, cover, leaving the lid slightly open, and simmer for about 1¼ hours until soft and thick. Remove from the heat.

3 Add the sugar, cardamom and saffron and stir well to mix thoroughly.

4 Return the pan to the heat and, stirring constantly, cook until thick and dry. Cool.

Dough
1 Sieve the flour and rub in the oil.

2 Add enough water to make a stiff dough. Knead for about 8–10 minutes until soft and smooth.

Filling
1 scant cup channa dal
about 3 cups water
1 cup sugar
½ tsp ground cardamom
½ tsp saffron
Dough
2 cups wholewheat flour
1 tbsp oil
about ½ cup hot water
ghee

3 Divide the dough into 10–12 balls.

4 Take a ball, flatten it on a slightly floured surface and roll into a round of 3 in across. Place 1 tbsp of the filling in the center and fold up the edges, enclosing the filling completely. Gently roll into a round 7 in across.

5 Place in a hot skillet and cook over a medium heat for 1–2 minutes each side until brown spots appear.

6 Brush with melted ghee and serve hot.

This can also be made with Toovar instead of Channa dal.

Doodh Pak

Gujarati-style creamed rice

5 cups milk
1 tbsp rice
2½ tbsp sugar
½ tsp ground cardamom
1 tbsp ground almonds

1 Bring the milk to a boil, stirring constantly.

2 Add the rice and sugar; stir to mix. Lower the heat, and, stirring occasionally, simmer until the milk has thickened and is reduced to about 2 cups.

3 Remove from the heat and stir in the cardamom and almonds, making sure no lumps form when the nuts are added.

Serve with hot Poori.

Shrikhand

Yogurt with saffron

2½ cups yogurt
¼ tsp saffron
1 tbsp warm milk
½ cup sugar
2 tbsp pistachio nuts, skinned and chopped

1 Put the yogurt into a cheesecloth bag and hang it up for 4–5 hours to get rid of the excess water.

2 Soak the saffron in the milk for 30 minutes.

3 Whisk together the drained yogurt, sugar and saffron milk until smooth and creamy.

4 Put in a dish and garnish with the nuts. Chill until set.

Any seasonal fruit may be added while whisking.

◆ *Nuts of many kinds (right) may be eaten as snacks and are often used to garnish a dish*

◆ **Shrikhand**/Yogurt with saffron *(below)* makes an intriguing and attractive finale to a meal — see page 161

TYPICAL MENUS

| Poori |
| Rice |
| Dhokla |
| Sambharia |
| Karhi |
| Kacha pakka kobi |
| Shrikhand |
| ★ ★ ★ |
| Rice |
| Bharaleli wangi |
| Jhinge batana |
| Aloo shak |
| Puran poori |

BREADS & RICE

An Indian meal should be eaten with a selection of breads and rice. Although some people might prefer chappatis and a few vegetables accompanied by dal, and others might prefer rice served with fish and a few fried vegetables, what actually happens in India is that families prepare meals from what is available in the region, and customs and eating habits follow suit. For example, the eastern region consumes more rice than the national average as this is where it grows and the northern region consumes more wheat for the same reason.

The variations of breads made from wholewheat flour are outstanding in their range of tastes. For example, consider the following type of bread: knead flour into a consistent dough, tear off a small piece, shape it into a ball and flatten the ball, roll into a circular shape not more than 4 in in diameter, with the help of a rolling pin. Finally, immerse the flattened ball in an already heated karai (deep frier) containing hot oil. A few seconds later, a fluffy golden brown Poori bounces to the surface, and the secret is to eat it immediately.

The second variation is the Chappati, which has very simple origins and is almost universal in its popularity within India. For this, the dough is rolled out to a circular shape not more than 8 in in diameter. The pancake is placed onto a "tava" (griddle) where it is cooked without any fat or oil.

The third variation is the Paratha, which is thicker than the Chappati but usually similar in size and shape. However, the method of preparing this bread differs from the others in that it has to be shallow fried in oil or fat and must be extremely crisp on the surface. The end result is a bit heavy but still very tasty.

We now move to the Naan, which is probably the best known of the Indian breads in the West. It tends to be served with other Tandoori dishes and has become very popular in Indian restaurants abroad. The Naan is different from other breads in that it is prepared in the tandoor, a clay oven, where the dough is slapped on the side of the oven. However, to be practical, I have given a recipe that can be prepared quite simply at home.

Cooking rice in India is something special. Rice can be boiled, fried or steamed, or a combination of the three. Try starting with plain boiled rice to accompany dal (lentils)—a simple but very popular dish—and move on to more elaborate biriyanis and pilafs.

Plain rice is for everyday meals, whereas fried rice, pilafs and biriyanis are for more festive occasions. Indians are a very hospitable people and they take pride in offering splendid meals when entertaining guests. Pilafs can be altered by adding one or more ingredients. For example, you can add peas to make a Pea pilaf, panir (curd cheese) to make a Panir pilaf, lamb to make a Lamb pilaf and so on.

A more unusual variation of rice is khichuri, a rice based preparation that does not look like rice when completed but more like a thick soup. It is rich and filling and popular during the monsoons when one might be reluctant to prepare a complicated meal. It is delicious accompanied by pickles and fried vegetables.

◆ *Delicate puffy breads like pale, creamy Lucchis (above) — see page 170 — and golden Pooris
(above right) — see page 178 — and rice are the perfect accompaniment to an Indian meal*

Batora

Yogurt bread

1 Sieve together the flour, baking powder and salt. Mix in the sugar.

2 Add the beaten egg and enough yogurt to form a stiff dough. Knead for 10–15 minutes until you have a soft, smooth dough. Cover with a cloth and let it rest for 3–4 hours.

3 Knead again on a floured surface for 5 minutes. Divide into 12–14 balls. Flatten the balls slightly between the palms.

4 Roll out on a floured surface into 5 in rounds.

5 Heat the oil in a karai or saucepan over a high heat. Fry the batora, pressing the middle with a slotted spoon so that it puffs up. Turn and cook the other side for a few seconds until lightly browned. Drain.

Serve with Kabli channa.

2 cups all-purpose flour
1½ tsp baking powder
½ tsp salt
1 tsp sugar
1 egg, beaten
about 3 tbsp yogurt
oil for deep frying

Chappati

Wholewheat flat bread

1 Sieve the flour and salt together. Add enough water to form a soft dough.

2 Knead for about 10 minutes until no longer sticky. Cover and set aside for 1 hour.

3 Divide the dough into 12–14 balls. Roll each ball into 6 in rounds on a floured surface. Flatten the balls slightly between the palms.

2½ cups wholewheat flour
½ tsp salt
about ¾ cup hot water
2 tbsp melted ghee (optional)

◇ **Chappatis**/Wholewheat flat breads *are delicious on their own, as a snack or with a curry*

4 Preheat the broiler until very hot.

5 Heat a skillet over a medium heat and place a chappati on it. Cook the chappati for about 2 minutes until brown spots appear. Turn and cook the other side.

6 Take the chappati and place it under the hot broiler for a few seconds so that it puffs up. Turn and cook the other side for a few seconds until it also puffs up.

7 Place the chappati in a dish and brush with a little melted ghee. Cover the chappatis as they are made and keep warm while cooking the others.

Gobi Paratha

BREAD

Layered bread with cauliflower

Filling

1 Grate the cauliflower, mix with the other ingredients and put aside.

Dough

1 Sieve the flour and salt together. Rub in the oil. Add enough water to form a stiff dough. Knead for about 10 minutes until you have a soft dough. Divide into 20 balls. Flatten the balls slightly between the palms.

2 Roll out 2 balls into 4 in rounds. Place about 1½–2 tbsp of the filling on 1 of the rounds, spreading it evenly. Place the other round over the filling, sealing the edges with a little water.

3 Roll out gently into 7 in rounds and be careful that no filling comes out. Roll out all the parathas in the same manner.

4 Heat a skillet over a medium heat. Place a paratha in the skillet and cook for about 1 minute until brown spots appear. Turn and cook the other side.

5 Add 2 tsp of ghee and cook for 2–3 minutes until golden brown. Turn and cook the other side; add more ghee if required. Make all the parathas in the same way.

The parathas can be cooked ahead of time and reheated in a hot, ungreased skillet for about 1 minute each side.

Serve warm with a Raita.

Filling
1 small cauliflower (about 1 lb), washed
1 tsp salt
½ tsp mango powder
½ tsp chili powder

Dough
3 cups flour
½ tsp salt
¼ cup oil
about ¾ cup hot water
ghee for frying

Lucchi

BREAD

Deep fried white bread

1 Sieve the flour and salt together. Rub in the oil.

2 Slowly add enough water to form a stiff dough. Knead for about 10 minutes until you have a soft, pliable dough.

3 cups flour
½ tsp salt
2 tbsp oil
about ¾ cup hot water
oil for deep frying

3 Divide the dough into about 40 small balls and flatten each ball.

4 Roll on a slightly oily surface into rounds of 4 in across (do not roll out all the balls at the same time as they tend to stick).

5 Heat oil in a karai or saucepan over a high heat. Put in a lucchi and press the middle with a slotted spoon to make it puff up. Turn and cook the other side for a few seconds. Drain and serve hot.

Mooli Paratha

BREAD

Layered bread with radish

Filling
1 Grate the white radish and mix with the other ingredients. Squeeze out all the water and discard it. Put aside.

Dough
1 Sieve together the flour and salt. Rub in the oil. Add enough water to make a stiff dough and knead for about 10 minutes to make it soft and pliable. Divide into 20 balls.

2 Roll out 2 balls into 4 in rounds. Flatten the balls slightly between the palms. Place about 1½–2 tbsp of the filling on 1 of the rounds, spreading it evenly. Place the other round over the filling, sealing the edges with a little water.

3 Roll out gently into 7 in rounds and be careful that no filling comes out. Roll out all the parathas in the same manner.

4 Heat a skillet over a medium heat. Place a paratha in the skillet and cook for about 1 minute, until brown spots appear. Turn and cook the other side.

5 Add 2 tsp of ghee and cook for 2–3 minutes until golden brown. Turn and cook the other side; add more ghee if required. Make all the parathas in the same way.

The parathas can be made ahead of time and reheated in a hot, ungreased skillet for about 1 minute each side.

Filling
1 lb white radish, washed and scraped
1 tsp salt
2–3 green chilies, finely chopped
½ tsp roasted cumin seeds, ground

Dough
3 cups flour
½ tsp salt
4 tbsp oil
about ¾ cup hot water
ghee for frying

MAKING A MOOLI PARATHA

1 *Remove the outer skin of the radish with a vegetable peeler.*
2 *Cut off both ends, using a sharp knife.*
3 *Grate the radish, fairly coarsely.*
4 *Squeeze the water from the grated radish and discard it.*
5 *Chop the chilies and mix with the radish, cumin and salt.*
6 *Roll out two 4in rounds of dough.*
7 *Spoon some of the filling on to the center of one round.*
8 *Brush the edge with water, to create a seal.*
9 *Add the top round of dough and roll gently.*

◇ **Mooli paratha**/Layered bread with radish

◇ *Appetizing, golden rounds of Naan are an ideal accompaniment for Tandoori meats*

Naan

Baked bread

1 Sieve together the flour, baking powder, salt, soda and sugar into a large bowl.

2 Next add the ghee and egg and stir thoroughly into the flour mixture.

3 Add enough milk to form a stiff dough. Knead for about 10 minutes.

4 Place a little ghee in a bowl. Put the dough in the bowl and roll it so that it becomes coated with ghee. Cover and let it rest for 3–4 hours.

2 cups flour
1 tsp baking powder
½ tsp salt
¼ tsp baking soda
½ tsp sugar
1 tbsp melted ghee
1 egg, lightly beaten
about ¼ cup milk
a little ghee

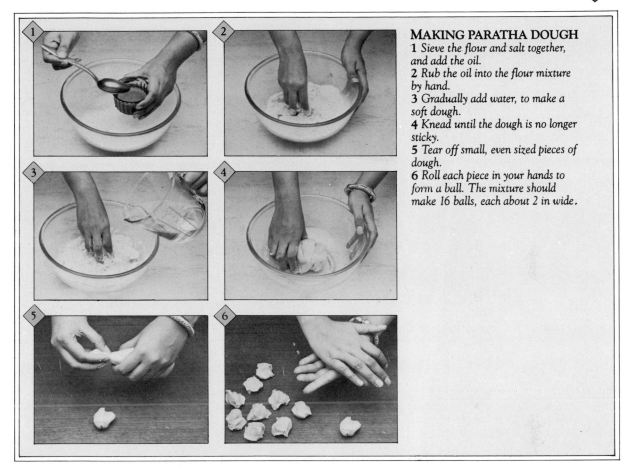

MAKING PARATHA DOUGH
1 *Sieve the flour and salt together, and add the oil.*
2 *Rub the oil into the flour mixture by hand.*
3 *Gradually add water, to make a soft dough.*
4 *Knead until the dough is no longer sticky.*
5 *Tear off small, even sized pieces of dough.*
6 *Roll each piece in your hands to form a ball. The mixture should make 16 balls, each about 2 in wide.*

5 Preheat the oven to 400°F. Heat 2 baking sheets.

6 Divide the dough into 7–8 portions. Take a portion and roll into a circle 7 in in diameter. Pull one end so that the dough takes on a tear shape, and flatten slightly between the palms. Roll out the rest of the dough in the same way.

7 Place the naans on the hot baking sheets and bake for 5–6 minutes.

8 Place under a very hot broiler for 15–20 seconds until brown spots appear.

Serve hot.

MAKING THE PARATHA

1 Sprinkle a little flour on a pastry board or worktop.

2 Flatten each dough ball with a rolling pin.

3 Roll until the circle is about 8 in across.

4 Brush the dough with ghee.

5 Fold the dough circle in half.

6 Brush a little more ghee on the top.

7 Fold the semicircle in half to make a triangle.

8 Roll the triangle out thinly on a floured surface, keeping its shape.

9 The paratha is now ready for frying.

Paratha

Layered bread

1 Sieve the flour and salt together. Rub in the oil.

2 Slowly add the water to form a soft dough. Knead for about 10 minutes until it is no longer sticky.

3 Divide the dough into 16 balls. Flatten a ball on a lightly floured surface and roll into a circle 8 in in diameter.

4 Brush a little ghee on this and fold in half, brush with a little more ghee and fold into a small triangle. Roll out the triangle quite thinly on the floured surface.

5 Heat a skillet over a medium heat and place a rolled triangle on it. Heat each side for 1 minute until brown specks appear. Put aside. Cook each triangle in this way.

6 Add the remaining ghee and gently fry the parathas, one at a time, for about 1 minute, turning once until golden brown.

While cooking the parathas, keep the fried ones warm by wrapping in aluminum foil.

3 cups flour
½ tsp salt
¼ cup oil
about ¾ cup hot water
3 heaped tbsp ghee, melted

◇ *The finished parathas are crispy and tasty*

◇ *Crispy pooris make a delightful accompaniment to vegetable curries.*

Poori

BREAD

Deep fried brown bread

1 Sieve together the flour and salt. Rub in the oil.

2 Add enough water to make a stiff dough. Put the dough on a floured surface and knead for about 10 minutes until soft and smooth.

3 Divide the mixture into 20 balls.

4 Take one ball at a time, flatten on a slightly oily surface and roll into rounds of 4 in across. (Do not stack the rolled pooris on top of one another as they might then stick together.)

2 cups wholewheat flour
½ tsp salt
2 tbsp oil
about ½ cup hot water
oil for deep frying

5 Heat the oil in a karai or saucepan until very hot. Add a rolled out poori; press the middle with a slotted spoon so that it puffs up. Quickly turn and cook the other side for a few seconds. Drain and serve hot.

Aloo Pillau

Potato pilaf

1 Make the coconut milk by blending together the creamed coconut and hot water. Put aside.

2 Chop the coriander leaves and throw away the lower stalks and roots. Wash them thoroughly.

3 Blend together the coriander leaves, shredded coconut, chilies, lemon juice, sugar, ½ tsp salt, garam masala and turmeric until you have a fine paste.

4 Parboil the potatoes. Drain and cool.

5 Take a potato and make 2 cuts like a cross coming about three quarters of the way down the length. Take care not to cut right through the potato. Cut all the potatoes in this way.

6 Fill each potato with a little of the coriander paste. If you have any paste left, rub it on to the potatoes.

7 Heat the oil over a medium high heat in a large saucepan. Add the cloves, and, after 3–4 seconds, add the onion and garlic and fry until the onion is lightly golden.

8 Add the rice and sauté for 2–3 minutes, stirring constantly.

9 Add the coconut milk and 1 tsp salt and bring to a boil. Add the potatoes, and when it comes to the boil again, lower heat to very low, cover and cook for about 20 minutes until all the water has been absorbed.

10 Fluff the rice with a fork before serving.

RICE

⅔ cup creamed coconut
2½ cups hot water
⅓ cup coriander leaves
1 tbsp shredded coconut
2 green chilies
2 tbsp lemon juice
½ tsp sugar
1½ tsp salt
½ tsp garam masala powder
¼ tsp ground turmeric
10–12 small new potatoes, washed and peeled
3 tbsp oil
2 cloves
1 medium onion, finely sliced
1 clove garlic, crushed
1¼ cups basmati rice, washed and drained

◇ **Aloo pillau**/Potato pilaf

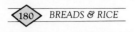

Ghee Bhat

RICE

Fried rice

1 Heat the ghee in a large skillet over a medium high heat. Add the bay leaves, cinnamon and cardamom and let them sizzle for a few seconds.

2 Add the onions and chilies and fry until the onions are golden brown.

3 Add the rice, sugar and raisins and continue frying until the rice is thoroughly heated.

This dish tastes even better if you use rice that was cooked a day earlier.

1½ cups basmati rice, cooked and cooled
3 tbsp ghee
2 bay leaves
2 in piece of stick cinnamon
4 cardamom pods
3 large onions, finely sliced
3 green chilies, cut lengthwise
1 tsp salt
½ tsp sugar
2 tbsp raisins (optional)

Khichuri

RICE

Rice with lentils

1 In a small pan, dry roast the moong dal over a medium heat until it turns light brown. Remove from the heat and wash thoroughly. Mix with the red lentils and put aside in a sieve to drain.

2 Heat the oil in a large saucepan over a medium heat. Add the bay leaves, cinnamon and cardamom and let them sizzle for a few seconds.

3 Add garlic, ginger and onion; fry until the onion is golden brown.

4 Add the turmeric, chili powder, salt, sugar and tomato; mix thoroughly. Add the rice and lentils and fry for 5–7 minutes, stirring constantly.

5 Add the water; when it starts to boil, lower heat and simmer for about 35–40 minutes.

6 Just before removing from the heat, add the green chilies.

Serve with melted ghee and anything fried.

⅓ cup moong dal
⅓ cup red lentils, washed
6 tbsp oil
2 bay leaves
2 in piece of stick cinnamon
4 cardamom pods
3 cloves garlic, crushed
1 in ginger, grated
1 large onion, finely sliced
1 tsp ground turmeric
½ tsp chili powder
1 tsp salt
⅓ tsp sugar
1 tomato, chopped
⅓ cup basmati rice, washed and drained
5½ cups water
3–4 green chilies, halved lengthwise

◇ **Matar pillau**/Pea pilaf *(top)* — *see page 182* ◇ **Sabzi ka pillau**/Vegetable pilaf *(above)* — *see page 183*

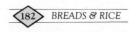

Matar Pillau

Pea pilaf

RICE

1½ cups basmati rice
2 large onions
6 tbsp oil
1 tbsp unsalted cashew nuts
3 cardamom pods
4 peppercorns
2 cloves
½ tsp cumin seeds
½ in ginger, grated
1 clove garlic, crushed
½ cup peas (fresh or frozen)
2½ cups water
1 tsp salt

1 Wash the rice in several changes of water and leave to soak in plenty of water for 30 minutes. Drain and leave the rice in a sieve for 30 minutes.

2 Peel the onions and finely slice 1½ onions and chop the remaining half.

3 Heat the oil, and fry the sliced onions until brown and crisp. Drain on paper towels and put aside.

4 In the remaining oil, fry the cashew nuts until golden brown. Drain on paper towels and put aside.

5 Add the cardamom, peppercorns, cloves and cumin, and let them sizzle for 5–6 seconds.

6 Add the ginger, garlic and chopped onion and stir fry until the onions are soft and transparent.

7 Add the peas and rice and sauté for 5 minutes. Add the water and salt and bring to a boil. Lower the heat to very low, cover and cook for 20 minutes until the water has been absorbed.

8 Fluff the rice gently with a fork and serve on a flat platter garnished with the fried onions and cashew nuts.

Sada Chawal (1)

Plain rice (1)

RICE

1½ cups basmati rice
3¾ cups cold water

1 Wash the rice 3 or 4 times in cold water. Drain.

2 Place the drained rice in a large saucepan and pour in the water. Bring to a boil rapidly over a high heat. Stir.

3 Lower heat to very low, cover and cook for about 20 minutes until all the water has been absorbed.

4 Fluff the rice with a fork and serve hot.

Sada Chawal (2)

Plain rice (2)

1½ cups basmati rice
12½ cups water

1 Wash the rice 3 or 4 times in cold water. Soak the rice in plenty of water for 1 hour. Drain.

2 Place the drained rice in a large saucepan, add the measured amount of water and bring to a boil over a high heat. Boil rapidly for about 5 minutes until the rice is cooked. Drain the rice, fluff it with a fork and serve hot.

Sabzi Ka Pillau

Vegetable pilaf

1½ cups basmati rice
5 tbsp ghee
2 tbsp unsalted cashew nuts
1 medium onion, finely chopped
½ in ginger, cut into very thin strips
1 cup French beans, cut into 1½ in lengths
2 small carrots, scraped and diced
½ cup peas
1 small red pepper, seeded and thinly sliced
3½ cups water
1½ tsp salt
1 tbsp coriander leaves

1 Wash the rice in several changes of water and leave in a sieve to drain thoroughly.

2 Heat the ghee in a large saucepan and fry the cashew nuts until golden. Drain and put aside.

3 In the remaining ghee, add the onion and ginger and fry until the onion is soft and transparent.

4 Add the rice and stir fry for 1–2 minutes. Add all the vegetables and mix with the onion and rice.

5 Add the water and salt and bring to a boil. Give it a good stir, lower the heat to very low, cover and cook for about 20 minutes until the rice and vegetables are tender and all the water is absorbed.

6 Garnish with the fried cashew nuts and coriander leaves.

ACCOMPANIMENTS

Indian meals are always enhanced by the side dishes. As a rule there is an assortment of relishes, such as pickles, chutneys and yogurt-based raitas. And to start and end a meal, there are pappadoms, crispy wafers which are widely available in shops and can be prepared by broiling or deep-frying.

In the Northern part of India, raitas (spiced yogurts) are very popular and the variations are infinite, limited only by the imagination of the person preparing the meal. One could start with an Onion Raita, an Orange Raita, a Banana Raita, a Cucumber Raita, a Tomato Raita and so on.

Chutneys are equally varied: popular Sweet mango chutney, Dhaniya (Coriander) chutney, Imli (Tamarind) chutney, Sweet date and prune chutney, Apricot chutney, Dried shrimp chutney or Dried fish chutney, and more. These all complement the meal and bring out the subtle taste of the other preparations.

Pickles in oil are particular favorites as they have a long shelf life; they are known as aachars. To prepare a pickle, you need an oil base or a vinegar base. For a vinegar based pickle you might add some chopped vegetables and spices to the vinegar and leave the mixture in a glass jar for a few months. Alternatively, carrots could be added, or cauliflowers, onions, chilies—whatever your personal preference is.

The oil commonly used for making pickles is mustard oil. To this you can add unripe mangoes, edible berries, chilies, lotus roots, drumsticks, lime and so on.

Such oil based pickles are always eaten with stuffed Parathas and no other accompaniments.

Yogurt based drinks, known as lassi, are made and enjoyed all over India. There are two kinds: sweet lassi and salted lassi. Lassi is a very soothing drink for the long, hot, severe Indian summers. Salted lassi may be mixed with various spices, and sweet lassi may contain nothing but sugar added to natural yogurt. But there are variations: in the Eastern region, for example, the people of Bengal add a squirt of Gondo lebu (Scented lime) to the sweet version.

Other aperitifs are Nimboopani, which is a drink with lime, a few spices, possibly including garam masala, a few ice cubes, and water to taste; and a digestive drink, Jeerapani, which is extremely spicy and a bit sour but is claimed to have a beneficial effect if you have eaten too much.

If you visit an Indian city during the summer months you are likely to see trolleys with colorful bottles of liquid being shunted around. The liquids are syrups, which are served with ice to soothe any parched passers-by. Another common sight is the ancient looking contraption of the grinding wheel that crushes sugar cane into a refreshing juice. It's almost worth a visit just to taste it.

Aam Ki Aachar

Mango pickle

10 green mangoes
½ tsp fenugreek seeds, ground
6 tbsp ground mustard
3 tsp salt
2 cups mustard oil
1 tsp asafetida
juice of 1 lime

1 Wash the mangoes and pat dry. Cut into 4 pieces, lengthwise. (Do not peel.)

2 Add the fenugreek, mustard and salt to the mangoes and mix well. Put aside for 15 minutes.

3 Heat the oil in a karai or saucepan over a medium heat. Add the asafetida and let it sizzle for 5–6 seconds.

4 Add the mangoes, and, stirring occasionally, fry until the mangoes are tender and well mixed.

5 Remove from the heat and, when it becomes lukewarm, stir in the lime juice.

Aamer Chutney

Mango chutney

4 green mangoes
2 tsp oil
1 tsp panch phoron
2 cardamom pods
1 in piece of stick cinnamon
2 cups water
½ tsp salt
4 tbsp sugar
1 tsp flour
2 tbsp milk

1 Wash the mangoes, and pat dry. Cut into 6 pieces, lengthwise.

2 Heat the oil in a saucepan over a medium high heat. Add the panch phoron, cardamom and cinnamon and let them sizzle for a few seconds.

3 Add the mangoes and stir fry for 2–3 minutes.

4 Add the water and salt and, when it starts to boil, add the sugar and stir in well. (Add more sugar if required.)

5 Cover, lower the heat and cook for 15–20 minutes until the mangoes are soft.

6 Meanwhile, mix the flour and milk together into a paste.

7 When the mangoes are soft, add the flour and milk mixture, stirring constantly to make sure that no lumps can form.

8 Remove from the heat and chill before serving.

◆ **Aam ki aachar**/Mango pickle *lends a spicy bite to milder curries and biriyanis.*

Aloo Raita

Yogurt with potatoes

1 Whisk the yogurt in a bowl until smooth.

2 Add the potatoes, onions, salt, pepper and cumin, and mix gently. Chill.

3 Serve sprinkled with the chili and coriander leaves.

2 cups yogurt
2½ cups boiled potatoes, diced into ¼ in cubes
1 small onion, finely chopped
½ tsp salt
¼ tsp ground black pepper
½ tsp ground roasted cumin
1 green chili, chopped
1 tbsp coriander leaves

Boondi Raita

Yogurt with boondi

1 Soak the boondi in a little cold water for 10–15 minutes.

2 Beat the yogurt in a bowl until smooth. Add the salt and chili powder and stir.

3 Gently squeeze the boondi to remove the water, add to the spiced yogurt and mix well. Chill. Before serving, sprinkle with the paprika and garam masala.

Boondi is fried gram flour batter, which can be bought at any Indian grocery store.

¾ cup boondi
1½ cups yogurt
½ tsp salt
½ tsp chili powder
pinch of paprika
pinch of garam masala powder

Hara Dhaniya Ki Chutney

Coriander chutney

1 Chop the sprigs of coriander and throw away the roots and lower stalks. Wash.

2 Blend the coriander with all the other ingredients until you have a smooth paste.

Can be stored in an airtight container in the refrigerator for one week.

Serve with any fried foods.

12–14 sprigs of coriander leaves
4 cloves garlic
3 tbsp shredded coconut
2 green chilies
2–3 tbsp lemon juice
½ tsp salt
¼ tsp sugar

Elaichi Chai

Cardamom tea

1 Put all the ingredients in a saucepan and bring to a boil.

2 Simmer for 4–5 minutes.

3 Strain and serve hot.

10–12 cardamom pods, slightly crushed
about 3 cups milk
4 tsp tea leaves or 3 tea bags
4 tsp sugar

Chaat Masala

Spices for garnishing

1 Mix all the ingredients together.

2 Store in an airtight bottle.

Sprinkle sparingly on fried foods.

2 tbsp black salt
2 tbsp roasted cumin seeds, ground
1 tsp ground ginger
1 tsp pepper
1 tsp chili powder

Imli Ki Chutney

Tamarind chutney

1 Soak the tamarind in the water for about 30 minutes. Squeeze well.

2 Strain and combine with the other ingredients. Chill.

⅔ cup tamarind
1½ cups hot water
¼ tsp chili powder
2 tbsp brown sugar
¼ tsp salt

Jeerapani

Cumin-flavored drink

1 Dissolve the cumin in the water and stir well.

2 Add the salt and mango powder and mix well.

This drink can be served as an aperitif or a digestive; it should be made 2 hours before needed and kept at room temperature.

3¾ cups cold water
1¼ tsp cumin seeds, roasted and ground
1 tsp black salt
½ tsp mango powder

◆ **Tamatar ki chutney**/Tomato chutney
and **Poodina ki chutney**/Mint chutney

(top left to right)

◆ **Hara dhaniya ki chutney**/Coriander chutney
(above) — *see page 188*

◆ **Aloo raita**/Yogurt with potatoes — *see page 188*

Kachumbar

Tomato, onion and cucumber relish

1 Mix all the ingredients together.

2 Chill for 2–3 hours before serving.

4 medium onions, finely chopped
2 large tomatoes, finely chopped
2 green chilies, finely chopped
5–6 tbsp coriander leaves, chopped
2–3 tbsp lime juice
1 tsp salt

Keera Raita

Yogurt with cucumber

1 In a bowl, whisk the yogurt until smooth.

2 Add all the other ingredients and stir well.

3 Chill.

1½ cups yogurt
1–2 green chilies, chopped
2 tbsp coriander leaves, chopped
½ cucumber, finely sliced
½ tsp chili powder
½ tsp ground roasted cumin
½ tsp salt

Metha Lassi

Sweetened yogurt drink

1 Whisk all the ingredients together until frothy.

2 Chill and serve.

1¼ cups yogurt
4¼ cups cold water
3 tsp sugar
few drops of rose water

Nimboopani

Lime drink

1 Squeeze the limes and strain the juice.

2 Dissolve the sugar in the water.

3 Stir in the lime juice and salt.

4 Add the crushed ice and serve.

3 limes
3¾ cups cold water
2 tbsp sugar
½ tsp salt
crushed ice

Lassi

Yogurt drink

1 Whisk the yogurt and water until frothy.

2 Add the salt and pepper. Stir well.

3 Chill and serve.

This is a very refreshing drink and enjoyed throughout India.

1 cup yogurt
5 cups cold water
¾ tsp salt
¼ tsp freshly milled black pepper

Khejurer Chutney

Date and prune chutney

1 Heat the oil in a saucepan over a medium high heat. Add the cardamom, cinnamon and red chilies and let them sizzle for 8–10 seconds.

2 Add the dates, prunes and raisins and stir fry for 3–4 minutes.

3 Add the water and salt and, when it comes to a boil, add the sugar and mix in well.

4 Lower the heat, cover and cook for about 15 minutes.

5 In the meantime mix the flour and milk to a smooth paste.

6 When the dates and prunes are tender, add the flour and milk paste, stirring constantly to make sure no lumps form.

7 Remove from the heat and chill before serving.

1 tbsp oil
2 cardamom pods
1 in piece of stick cinnamon
2 dried red chilies
⅔ cup dates
1⅓ cups prunes
1 tbsp raisins
1½ cups water
½ tsp salt
3 tbsp sugar
1 tsp flour
2 tbsp milk

Poodina Ki Chutney

Mint chutney

1 Blend all the ingredients together until you have a smooth paste.

Can be stored in an airtight container in the refrigerator for one week only.

¼ cup mint leaves, washed
¼ cup tamarind juice
2 tbsp chopped onions
2 cloves garlic
¾ in ginger
2–3 green chilies
½ tsp salt
½ tsp sugar

Pyaz Ki Salad

Onion salad

1 Mix all the ingredients together and set aside for at least one hour.

Serve with any kebobs.

1 large onion, finely sliced
1 tsp salt
1 tbsp lemon juice

Sonth

Spicy tamarind chutney

1 Soak the tamarind in the water for 30 minutes. Squeeze well and strain.

2 In a saucepan, place the tamarind juice, sugar, salt, chili powder, ginger, dates and raisins and bring to a boil, stirring constantly, over a medium heat. Cook until thick.

3 Remove from the heat, sprinkle the ground cumin on the mixture and chill until required.

⅓ cup dried tamarind
1 cup hot water
2½ tsp sugar
½ tsp salt
½ tsp chili powder (optional)
½ in ginger, grated
1 tbsp dates, finely chopped
1 tbsp raisins, finely chopped
½ tsp roasted cumin seeds, ground

◆ **Metha lassi**/Sweetened yogurt drink — *see page 192*

FOREIGN INFLUENCES

Through the centuries India has attracted foreign peoples from all over the world. Different movies inspired different peoples — trade with India brought the British, Jews came to escape persecution in other lands, the Parsees fled from Persia to India in the eighteenth century, and the Portuguese arrived under the leadership of Vasco da Gama, hungry for adventure and attracted by the bounteous natural resources of the sub-continent. All of these peoples have left their mark on the cuisine of India, adapting their favorite native recipes to the ingredients and cooking methods they found in different regions of India.

Many other peoples have, at one time or another, occupied and influenced the subcontinent. The British set up trade with India early in the seventeenth century, but it was not until 200 years later that they achieved control of the country. They did not interfere with the cultural or religious beliefs of the Indian people but concentrated their efforts on trade and administration.

Nonetheless, the British adapted many Indian dishes to their own taste. Mulligatawny soup is the best known, although it has many variations. It can be made with a lentil base or a coconut milk base. The soup contains a few small pieces of chicken and is served with a bowl of rice and a slice of lime. The best way to eat it is to savor a little rice with each spoonful of soup and squeeze a few drops of lime on it to taste. It can be served as an appetizer or as a light meal on its own.

Another dish with a strong influence from the days of the Raj is the Jhal frezie. This is usually made with leftover meat, poultry and vegetables. The meat and vegetables are fried with onions and a little spice. The dish is normally eaten with a pilaf (a rice dish) or Paratha (Layered bread).

The Muslim influence in Indian non-vegetarian cookery is still felt in certain areas of India, especially in the North and in cities such as Lucknow in Uttar Pradesh and Hyderabad in Andhra Pradesh. I have included a few of these recipes in their relevant chapters.

India also has a small Jewish community dating back to 587 BC. Their numbers have diminished drastically, however, most having moved to Israel. The Jewish settlement in Cochin in the state of Kerala was the largest, although it probably numbers less than fifty now. A synagogue was built there in 1567, which will eventually be turned into a museum. There has been no rabbi there within living memory, so all the Jewish elders of Cochin are qualified to perform religious ceremonies and marriages. Although the number of Jews in India is dwindling, elements of Jewish cuisine can still be found in the area.

A very different influence on India was provided by the Parsees. This was a Zoroastrian community that fled from Persia in the eighth century because of Muslim persecution. The Parsees first settled in Gujarat in Western India. In the late eighteenth century their skills as traders and ship builders proved useful to the British, at the time involved in the Napoleonic Wars. In fact, the Parsees proved so valuable to the British government that it encouraged the East India Company to keep ploughing resources into the Parsee settlement in Bombay. Possibly one of the factors influencing the success of the Parsees was that they had no inhibitions on matters of caste or diet.

The Parsees flourished as traders and in so doing became more westernized, sponsoring many cultural activities that heightened India's awareness of Western music, opera and ballet. In terms of cuisine, theirs is an assimilation of Persian and Indian cooking, the most renowned recipe being Dhansak (Meat with lentils), which should be eaten with a specially prepared brown rice to achieve a truly authentic texture and flavor.

India, with its wealth of natural resources, has always been a dream for adventurers and explorers. Consider Vasco da Gama, whose ship arrived at the coast of Kerala in the late fifteenth century, having traveled all the way from Portugal. His aim was solely to trade and to improve his standing at home, both of which he achieved. However, the Portuguese had greater ambitions. They wanted to control the spice route from the East, and Goa was a perfect location for this. By the turn of the century, the Portuguese had captured Goa and become the chief spice traders as well as a powerful force in India. They spread Christianity and in the process destroyed many existing temples, replacing them with Western churches and monasteries.

The Portuguese finally left India in 1961 after which the people of Goa, the Goans, became members of the Republic of India. The Goans are a very hard working race and are proud of their interesting heritage. Their influence on Indian cooking is distinctive. The most popular Goan dish is Pork vindaloo—an extremely hot combination of roasted and ground spices, which are soaked in vinegar or wine and mixed with the meat before cooking. I have included a Shrimp vindaloo recipe (*see page 214*); you can also try it with duck. Sorpotel is another traditional Goan dish which is normally made with pork, using both the liver and the blood. I have omitted the blood in my recipe (*see page 213*) and am certain you will find the results delicious.

Goa differs from the other coastal areas of India because of its strong Portuguese influence. The beautiful beaches are more to Western tastes and people visit Goa as a resort combining the best of both worlds—the exotic East combined with the modern West. Thus, tourism booms for Goa with its golden beaches, coconut plantations and lush paddy fields.

Fishermen set out at dawn or dusk and return loaded with fresh fish, which you can buy then and there. The fish that do not sell are left on the beach to dry. Coconuts grow in abundance and every part of the coconut is used by the locals. The coconut milk is used for cooking, the flesh is used for garnishing and the oil derivative makes an excellent cooking medium. Along with their staple diet of coconut, the fishermen eat rice and fish.

Goa has a unique type of alcohol based drink called feni, flavored with either cashew nuts or coconuts, and you can buy it ready made. It's certainly worth a try one moonlit evening on the beach!

St Francis Xavier arrived in Goa in 1542 and devoted his life to spreading Christianity there. After his death, it was found that his body remained fresh and lifelike, seemingly a miracle. The body is now shown to the public every ten years and to some fervent believers the fact that his body has still not decomposed is proof of his holiness.

Like the Portuguese, the Dutch and the French also traded in India, but they left none of their influence behind. Those peoples who did leave their mark—whether British, Jewish, Parsee or Portuguese—have enriched rather than adulterated India's culinary heritage, as the diversity of the following recipes demonstrates.

Murgh Jhal Frezie

Chicken with onions and vegetables

1 Chop 2 of the onions and slice the other.

2 Heat the oil in a large skillet over a medium heat and fry the chopped onions, garlic and ginger until lightly golden.

3 Add the chicken, sliced onions, green chilies, turmeric, chili powder, vegetables and salt and fry for about 10–12 minutes until the vegetables are tender.

4 Add the catsup and tomato and fry for 1 minute more.

Serve with a Pilaf or Paratha.

3 medium onions
2–3 tbsp oil
2 cloves garlic, crushed
½ in ginger, grated
1 lb/2 cups chicken, boneless boiled or leftover roast cut into small cubes
3–4 green chilies, chopped
good pinch of ground turmeric
pinch of chili powder
¾ cup mixed vegetables, frozen
1 tsp salt
1 tbsp tomato catsup
1 small tomato, cut into 8 pieces

Mulligatawny

Curried soup

1 Skin the chicken and cut into small pieces.

2 Place the pieces of chicken, water and salt in a large saucepan and bring to a boil over a medium high heat.

3 Lower the heat and simmer until it has reduced to about 1¾ cups.

4 In the meantime, dry roast the cumin, coriander and channa dal until they are a few shades darker.

5 Grind the dry roasted spices with the poppy seeds, garlic, ginger, peppercorns, turmeric and green chilies.

6 Remove the chicken pieces from the broth, bone them and shred into very small pieces.

7 Add the ground spices to the broth and mix well. Sieve this mixture and put aside.

8 In a large saucepan, heat the ghee and fry the onion until lightly golden.

1 breast of chicken
about 6 cups water
1 tsp salt
1 tsp cumin seeds
2 tsp coriander seeds
1 tbsp channa dal
1 tbsp poppy seeds
3 cloves garlic
½ in ginger
5 peppercorns
½ tsp ground turmeric
2–3 green chilies
1 tbsp ghee
1 small onion, finely sliced
2 cups coconut milk

9 Add the spiced broth and cook for 2–3 minutes over a medium heat. Lower the heat to medium low.

10 Add the coconut milk and pieces of chicken and cook for 5–10 minutes. If the soup is too thick, add a little more water or coconut milk.

Serve with a bowl of boiled rice, slices of lime and chopped green chilies, to be sprinkled on according to taste.

Aloo Makalla

JEWISH

Deep fried potatoes

1 lb potatoes, small and longish
¼ tsp ground turmeric
1 tsp salt
oil for deep frying

1 Peel the potatoes and prick them all over with a fork.

2 Parboil the potatoes with the turmeric and salt. Drain.

3 Heat the oil until hot, and deep fry the potatoes until lightly golden.

4 Remove the oil from the heat and leave the potatoes in the hot oil for about 20 minutes. Remove the potatoes.

5 Heat the oil again until very hot. Gently add the potatoes and fry until crisp and browned. Serve immediately.

Beet Khuta

JEWISH

Chicken with beets

2½ lb chicken, skinned and cut into 10–12 pieces
4 medium onions, sliced
1 in ginger, grated
2 cloves garlic, crushed
3¾ cups water
4 cooked beets, halved and sliced
4 medium tomatoes, halved and sliced
4–5 green chilies
1 tsp sugar
4–5 tbsp mint leaves
juice of 2 lemons

1 Place the chicken, onions, ginger and garlic in a saucepan with the water and bring to the boil.

2 Boil the chicken until tender.

3 Add the beets, tomatoes and chilies and stir. Cook for about 15 minutes.

4 Add the sugar and mint, and cook for a further 10 minutes.

5 Squeeze the juice of the lemons and serve with rice.

◆ **Mulligatawny**/Curried soup *(opposite) is part of the British culinary legacy — see page 200*

◆ **Murgh jhal frezie**/Chicken with onions and vegetables *(above) is another popular dish from the days of the Raj — see page 200*

Chuteraney

Sweet and sour lamb

½ cup oil
1½ lb/3 cups onions, halved and sliced
½ tsp chili powder
¼ tsp ground turmeric
1 in ginger, grated
1½ lb/4 cups lamb, cut into 1 in cubes
3 medium tomatoes, chopped
about 2 cups water
3 tbsp vinegar
2 tsp sugar
1 tsp salt

1 Heat the oil in a saucepan over a medium high heat and fry the onions until golden brown.

2 Add the chili, turmeric and ginger and, stirring constantly, fry for 1–2 minutes.

3 Add the lamb and tomatoes and continue to fry for another 8–10 minutes, until the meat is browned.

4 Add the water, stir well and bring to a boil.

5 Lower heat, cover and cook for about 45 minutes.

6 Add the vinegar, sugar and salt and cook for another 15 minutes.

Akuri

Scrambled eggs

6 tbsp oil
2 medium onions, finely chopped
½ in ginger, grated
1 clove garlic, crushed
½ tsp ground turmeric
½ tsp chili powder
1½ tsp salt
3 medium tomatoes, finely chopped
8 eggs, lightly beaten
2 tbsp coriander leaves, chopped
2–3 green chilies, chopped

1 Heat the oil in a large skillet over a medium high heat. Add the onions, ginger and garlic and fry until golden.

2 Add the turmeric, chili powder and salt and mix with the onions.

3 Add the tomatoes, and continue to fry until the tomatoes are soft and tender. Lower the heat to medium low.

4 Remove from the heat and add the eggs, coriander leaves and green chilies. Return to the heat and, stirring gently, cook until scrambled.

Serve with hot toast or fried bread.

Bhindi Per Eda

Eggs on okra

1 lb okra
4 tbsp oil
2 medium onions, finely sliced
2 green chilies, chopped
1 tsp salt
4 eggs

1 Wash the okra and dry thoroughly. Cut off the stalk end and slice the okra into 1 in pieces.

2 Heat the oil in a skillet and add the onions, okra, chilies and salt and fry for about 10 minutes until the okra is tender.

3 Place in an ovenproof dish. Break the eggs on top of the okra so that it is completely covered and bake in a preheated oven at 350°F for about 15 minutes until the eggs are set.

Dhansak

Meat with lentils

1¾ cups red lentils, washed
2 cups pumpkin, peeled and cut into 1 in pieces
2 cups doddy, peeled and cut into 1 in pieces
1 medium potato, peeled and diced
1 medium onion, chopped
1 tsp ground turmeric
2 tsp salt
3 medium tomatoes, chopped
1½ lb/4 cups lamb, cut into 1 in cubes
¼ cup oil
1 in ginger, grated
3 cloves garlic, crushed
3 dried red chilies, ground
1½ tsp ground coriander
1½ tsp ground cumin
½ tsp ground mustard
½ tsp fenugreek seeds, ground
1½ tsp sambar powder

1 Place the lentils, pumpkin, doddy, potato, onion, turmeric and salt in a large saucepan, and add enough water to cover it by 1½ in.

2 Boil the lentils and simmer until tender. Add the tomatoes and cook for a further 10 minutes.

3 Pass the lentils and vegetables through a sieve and put aside.

4 Boil the meat in a little water for about 45 minutes until tender. Put aside.

5 Heat the oil in a large saucepan over a medium heat. Add all the spices and fry for 1–2 minutes, stirring constantly, so that they do not stick. If necessary, sprinkle on a few drops of water to prevent the spices from burning.

6 Add the lentils and lamb and simmer on a low heat for about 30 minutes. (The lentils should be quite thick.)

Serve with brown rice, Kebobs and Kachumbar.

Doddy is a vegetable widely available in Indian supermarkets and grocers' stores.

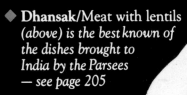

◆ **Dhansak**/Meat with lentils *(above) is the best known of the dishes brought to India by the Parsees — see page 205*

◆ **Beet khuta**/Chicken *with beets (right) comes from Cochin, where a Jewish community once flourished — see page 201*

◆ **Kabab**/Lamb kebob *is another dish of Parsee*
origin — see page 208

Kabab

Lamb kebab

1 lb/2 cups lamb, finely ground
2 medium potatoes, peeled and quartered
1 tsp salt
about ½ cup water
1 large slice of white bread
about ¼ cup milk
¾ in ginger, grated
2 cloves garlic, crushed
2–3 green chilies, chopped
1 egg
oil for deep frying

1 Place the ground lamb, potatoes, salt and water in a saucepan and bring to a boil. Simmer for about 20 minutes until the meat and potatoes are tender. Drain and cool.

2 Soak the bread in the milk for 5 minutes. Squeeze out the extra milk and add the boiled ground lamb and potatoes.

3 Mix thoroughly with your hands or in the food processor.

4 Add all the other ingredients and mix well.

5 Form into small balls the size of a walnut and deep fry in hot oil for about 1 minute.

If the mixture is too soft when all the ingredients are combined, add a few freshly made breadcrumbs.

Machi No Sas

Fish with eggs

2–3 medium tomatoes
1½ lb white fish
½ cup oil
3 medium onions, finely chopped
3 cloves garlic, crushed
1½ tsp chili powder
1½ tsp ground cumin
1½ tsp salt
6 eggs
about ⅓ cup vinegar
1 tbsp sugar
½ cup coriander leaves, chopped
3–4 green chilies, chopped

1 Skin the tomatoes and purée them in a food processor or blender.

2 Wash the fish and cut into 8–10 pieces. Pat dry with paper toweling.

3 Heat the oil in a large skillet and fry the onions and garlic until the onions are golden.

4 Add the chili powder, cumin and salt and fry with the onions for about 1 minute.

5 Add the pieces of fish and the tomato purée. Stir gently.

6 When it starts to boil, lower the heat, cover and cook for about 10–12 minutes until the fish is tender.

7 Carefully remove the pieces of fish and put aside. Let the sauce cool down completely.

8 Beat the eggs with the vinegar and sugar and pour into the cold sauce.

9 Heat the sauce again over a very gentle heat, stirring constantly, until the sauce is thickened.

10 Add the pieces of fish and cook for 1–2 minutes more.

11 Remove from the heat and garnish with the coriander leaves and green chilies. Serve immediately.

Cook gently after adding the egg mixture, or the eggs might curdle.

Patra Ni Machi

PARSEE

Fish wrapped in banana leaves

1½ lb pomfret or any white fish, cleaned
½ tsp salt
14–16 sprigs of coriander leaves
⅓ cup coconut, grated
4 green chilies
¾ tsp cumin seeds
¾ tsp sugar
½ tsp salt
juice of 1 lime
2–3 banana leaves, washed and dried
string for tying parcels
oil for shallow frying

1 Wash the fish and cut into 8–10 pieces. Rub in the salt and put aside.

2 Wash and chop the coriander leaves, discarding the lower stalks and roots.

3 In a food processor or liquidizer, blend together the coriander leaves, coconut, chilies, cumin seeds, sugar, salt and lime juice into a fine paste. (If necessary, add a little water.)

4 Spread the chutney on both sides of the pieces of fish.

5 Cut the banana leaves into sizes suitable for wrapping a piece of fish. Tie with some string.

6 Heat the oil in a large skillet and fry the parcels over a medium low heat until the leaves turn brownish black. Turn the parcels over carefully and fry until the leaves turn dark brown.

7 Drain, remove the string and place the parcels on a flat dish. The parcels should be unwrapped at the table (the leaves should not be eaten).

If banana leaves are not available, wrap the pieces of fish with the chutney spread on them in aluminum foil and bake in a pre-heated oven at 375°F for about 25–30 minutes.

Sali Murghi

Chicken with fried potatoes

1 Skin the chicken and cut into 8 pieces. Wash and put to one side.

2 Wash the potatoes, peel and cut into julienne strips. Soak in cold salted water for about 30 minutes.

3 Heat 6 tbsp of oil in a saucepan over a medium high heat and fry the onions, ginger and garlic, stirring constantly, until the onions are golden brown.

4 Add the chili and salt, mix with the onions; fry for about 30 seconds.

5 Add the chicken pieces and continue to fry for 8–10 minutes.

6 Add the water. Bring to a boil. Lower the heat, cover and cook for about 20–25 minutes until the chicken is tender and the gravy thickened.

7 Add the garam masala and cook for a further 2–3 minutes.

8 While the chicken is cooking, drain the potatoes and dry on paper toweling.

9 Heat the oil for deep frying, and fry the potatoes until golden brown and crisp.

10 Arrange the chicken on a flat dish and place the fried potatoes around it.

2½ lb chicken
2 lb potatoes
6 tbsp oil
3 large onions, finely sliced
½ in ginger, grated
2 cloves garlic, crushed
1½ tsp chili powder
1 tsp salt
1 cup water
1 tsp garam masala powder
oil for deep frying

Vagharela Chawal

Brown rice

1 Wash the rice in several changes of water. Drain.

2 Brown the sugar in a small pan over a medium heat. When dark brown, add 1¼ cups of the water, cumin and cinnamon and cook for 5 minutes.

1½ cups basmati rice
1 tsp sugar
3¾ cups cold water
½ tsp cumin seeds
1 in piece of stick cinnamon

3 Place the cleaned rice in a large saucepan, add the browned water and the remaining water and bring to a boil over a high heat.

4 Lower the heat to very low, cover tightly and cook for about 20 minutes until all the water has evaporated.

5 Fluff the rice gently with a fork.

Serve with Dhansak, Kabab and Kachumbar

Goan Channa Dal

PORTUGUESE

Goan-style lentils

1 scant cup channa dal
5 cups water
½ tsp ground turmeric
⅔ cup coconut, grated
1 tsp whole coriander seeds
1 tsp whole cumin seeds
3 cardamom pods
1 in piece of stick cinnamon
2 cloves
½ in ginger
3 cloves garlic
3–4 dried red chilies
½ cup tamarind juice
3 tbsp oil
6–8 curry leaves
1 small onion, finely chopped
1½ tsp salt
2–3 tbsp coriander leaves, chopped

1 Wash the channa dal in several changes of water.

2 Add the dal and turmeric to the measured amount of water in a large saucepan and bring to a boil over a medium high heat. Throw away any scum.

3 Lower the heat, cover the pan, leaving the lid slightly open, and simmer for about 1¼ hours until the dal is soft.

4 While the dal is cooking, dry roast the coconut, coriander, cumin, cardamom, cinnamon and cloves over a medium heat until they have turned a few shades darker and there is a nice aroma. Grind to a fine powder.

5 In a food processor or liquidizer, blend together the ginger, garlic, chilies, tamarind juice and the ground spices until smooth.

6 Heat the oil in a large saucepan over a medium high heat. Add the curry leaves and let them sizzle for about 10 seconds.

7 Add the onion and fry until golden. Lower heat slightly.

8 Add the blended mixture and salt, and cook for 2–3 minutes. Add the cooked dal and mix. Let it come to a boil and cook for a further 5–7 minutes. Garnish with the coriander leaves.

If the dal gets too thick add a little water.

Goan Jhinge Mooli

Goan shrimp curry

1 Soak the tamarind in 1¼ cups of the hot water and leave aside for 30 minutes.

2 Make the coconut milk by blending the creamed coconut and the remaining water in a blender or food processor.

3 Shell the shrimp, leaving the tails on. Make a small cut on the back and remove the black vein. Wash and pat dry.

4 Mix the cumin, turmeric, garlic, ginger and red chilies to a paste.

5 Squeeze the soaked tamarind well to draw out all the pulp. Strain. Mix the juice with the coconut milk, the onion, salt, green chilies and the paste.

6 Place the mixture in a saucepan over a medium high heat and bring to a boil. Boil for about 10 minutes.

7 Add the shrimp. Bring to a boil once more. Lower heat to medium and cover and cook for about 30 minutes, until the shrimp are tender and the gravy has thickened.

½ cup dried tamarind
2¼ cups hot water
⅓ cup creamed coconut
1 lb jumbo shrimp
1½ tsp ground cumin
good pinch of ground turmeric
4 cloves garlic, crushed
½ in ginger, grated
6 dried red chilies, ground
1 onion, finely sliced
1 tsp salt
3 green chilies, slit lengthwise

Shakuti

Lamb with coconut

1 Take three quarters of the grated coconut and blend with 1 cup of the hot water. Strain and keep the thick milk aside. Blend the pulp again with the remaining water, and strain again to extract the thin milk.

2 Dry roast the remaining coconut with the cumin, coriander, peppercorns, red chilies, poppy seeds, cinnamon, cardamom, and cloves over a medium heat, stirring constantly until the coconut is golden.

3 Grind the roasted coconut and spices with the garlic and ginger to a fine paste. (If you need to add any liquid during grinding, add a little of the thin coconut milk.)

1 fresh coconut, grated
2½ cups hot water
1 tsp cumin seeds
1 tbsp coriander seeds
8 peppercorns
10 dried red chilies
1½ tbsp poppy seeds
1 in piece of stick cinnamon
3 cardamom pods, skinned
3 cloves
4 cloves garlic
¾ in ginger
6 tbsp oil
2 large onions, halved and then finely sliced

4 Heat the oil in a large saucepan over a medium high heat. Add the onions and fry, stirring constantly, until lightly golden.

5 Add the lamb and brown all over, turning it frequently and reducing the heat if necessary.

6 Add the turmeric, salt and ground paste and mix thoroughly with the meat.

7 Carefully add the thin milk and bring to a boil. Cover, lower the heat and cook for about 45 minutes.

8 Add the tamarind juice and simmer for a further 10 minutes.

9 Add the thick coconut milk and simmer for 5 minutes more. Garnish with the coriander leaves and serve hot.

2⅔ cups lamb, cut into 1 in cubes
1 tsp ground turmeric
1½ tsp salt
¼ cup tamarind juice
2 tbsp coriander leaves, chopped

Sorpotel

Spicy pork

1 Grind together the chilies, coriander, cumin, mustard, peppercorns, cloves and cinnamon until finely ground.

2 Mix the ground spice with the onion, chilies, ginger, garlic and vinegar. Add to the meat and liver and mix well. Put aside for 1 hour.

3 Heat the oil in a large saucepan over a medium high heat. Add the meat mixture, turmeric and salt and sauté for about 15 minutes until the oil floats on top.

4 Add the water and tamarind juice. Bring to a boil, cover and cook on a gentle heat for about 1 hour, until the pork is tender.

Serve with rice.

10 dried red chilies
½ tsp coriander seeds
1 tsp cumin seeds
1 tsp mustard seeds
½ tsp peppercorns
4 cloves
1 in piece of stick cinnamon
1 large onion, finely sliced
3 green chilies, chopped
½ in ginger, grated
6 cloves garlic, crushed
6 tbsp vinegar
1½ lb/4 cups pork, cut into very small cubes
½ lb/1 cup liver, cut into ½ in pieces
6 tbsp oil
½ tsp turmeric
1 tsp salt
1¼ cups water
½ cup tamarind juice

Vindaloo

Shrimp vindaloo

1 lb jumbo shrimp
4 dried red chilies
6 black peppercorns
1 tsp coriander seeds
1 tsp cumin seeds
¾ in ginger, grated
3 cloves garlic, crushed
¼ cup white vinegar
1 tsp salt
¼ cup oil
2 medium onions, finely sliced

1 Shell the shrimp, leaving the tails on. Make a little incision along the back and remove the black vein. Wash and pat dry.

2 Dry roast the chilies, peppercorns, coriander and cumin until they turn a few shades darker and emit a pleasant aroma. Grind to a fine powder.

3 Mix the powder to a paste with the ginger, garlic, vinegar and salt.

4 Rub the paste in to the shrimp.

5 Heat the oil and fry the onions until golden. Let the oil and onions become cold together.

6 Add the onions and oil to the shrimp. Mix well and marinate for 3–4 hours.

7 Place the shrimp with all the marinade in a large saucepan over a medium high heat. When it starts to boil, lower heat to very low, cover and cook for 30–40 minutes, stirring occasionally, until the shrimp are tender. (If necessary add a little water to make a thickish gravy.)

ENGLISH & HINDI TERMS

Aachar	Pickle	**Lasun**	Garlic
Adrak	Ginger	**Laung**	Cloves
Amchoor	Dried mango powder	**Machi**	Fish
Atta	Wholewheat flour	**Maida**	Flour
Badam	Almonds	**Masala**	Spices
Chawal	Rice	**Methi**	Fenugreek
Chawara	Dates, dried	**Mithai**	Sweetmeats
Chilka	Skin	**Moongphali**	Peanuts
Dahi	Yogurt	**Murghi**	Chicken
Dalchini	Cinnamon	**Namak**	Salt
Dhaniya	Coriander	**Naram**	Tender
Dudh	Milk	**Nariyal**	Coconut
Elaichi	Cardamom	**Nimboo**	Lime
Gosht	Meat	**Panir**	Cheese
Gur	Molasses	**Phal**	Fruit
Haldi	Turmeric	**Pista**	Pistachio nuts
Hara	Green	**Piyaz**	Onion
Hing	Asafetida	**Poha**	Pounded rice
Imli	Tamarind	**Poodina**	Mint
Jeera	Cumin	**Ras**	Syrup
Jhinga	Shrimp or jumbo shrimp	**Roti**	Bread
Kaju	Cashew nuts	**Rye**	Mustard
Kalimirchi	Pepper	**Sabji**	Vegetable
Kalonji	Onion seeds	**Sabut**	Whole chilies
Kesar	Saffron	**Sada**	Plain
Khatta	Sour	**Sarson**	Mustard
Khoa	Dried, coagulated milk	**Suji**	Semolina
Khuskhus	Poppy seed	**Sukha**	Dry
Kishmish	Raisins	**Tej patta**	Bay leaves
Lal Mirchi	Chili, dry, red	**Vark**	Silver leaf

WEIGHTS & MEASURES

Most cooks in India do not weigh or measure ingredients when cooking. If you ask someone for the recipe of a dish you have enjoyed in their house, you may be told just the ingredients, and by trial and error you will come to make a dish that will suit your taste. There is no one recipe for making one particular dish: the ingredients may be the same but the amounts will vary considerably.

The amounts given in the recipes will, I hope, suit many people's taste but you can adjust the amounts as you become familiar with Indian styles of cooking and with the flavors of each individual dish. The measurement of spices is a particularly flexible area: a few dishes will be spoiled if they are made so mild that they lose their savor, or so hot that the delicate flavors are overwhelmed but, by and large, Indian dishes benefit from an individual interpretation.

The same rule of thumb applies if you want to reduce the quantities — the ones given will feed four to six people. Experiment to achieve a balance of ingredients that suits your own palate and those of your guests.

For a greater number of people, it is far more interesting and appealing to increase the number of dishes to be served than to increase the quantities of a single dish. Choose dishes that complement one another: violent clashes of flavor tend to reduce the diner's appreciation of individual dishes. Use the typical menus for the cuisine of each region given at the end of each recipe section to assist you in choosing suitable combinations.

INDEX

Page numbers in *italic* refer to the illustrations